The manager's guide to
international labour standards

The manager's guide to international labour standards

Alan Gladstone

Management Development Series No. 23
International Labour Office   Geneva

ISBN 92-2-105412-8
ISSN 0074-6703

First published 1986

ILO publications can be obtained through major booksellers or ILO local offices in many countries, or direct from ILO Publications, International Labour Office, CH-1211 Geneva 22, Switzerland. A catalogue or list of new publications will be sent free of charge from the above address.

Contents

Introduction

Probably many managers, if they ponder the question at all, tend to consider international labour standards bearing directly or indirectly on the management function as possible sources of interference with their carrying out of that function. The fact is, of course, that most managers are largely unaware, or only vaguely aware, of international labour standards. But beyond this there is the consideration that such standards, in addition to being a basis for regulation of certain managerial action, can also, if better known, provide guidance and inspiration for managers. Indeed, in many cases, international labour standards can result in substantially improved management practice.

It is in this spirit that the present guide is conceived. It is important to recognise that international labour standards reflect a consensus among employers as well as between them and governments and trade unions. Moreover, they are prepared by technical experts on the basis of intensive study and survey of best prevailing practices. As such, they are a rich source, if not a storehouse, of practical advice and suggestions that managers can take into account in their day-to-day activities, to their own benefit and that of their enterprises.

This educational dimension of international labour standards goes further than suggesting specific tools, approaches and policies for management. There is also the very important idea that managers can profit from this guide by familiarising themselves with recognised and accepted international labour and personnel practices in a number of domains of interest to them. Thus, even where a discussion of certain of the selected standards concerned is not of immediate practical import to the manager's daily work, it should nevertheless give him a useful perspective on the subject-matter in question, a perspective which can broaden his horizons, sharpen his awareness of possible future problems and ultimately be of use when he is faced with a specific problem. For example, a manager may not have been called upon, by reason of the state of the economy or of his enterprise, to envisage appropriate and effective measures to deal with redundancy, and there may be no reason for him to believe that he will have to deal with such a situation in the future (moreover there may be no relevant rules that are obligatory in this particular area). Nevertheless, a knowledge that there are certain procedures, practices and measures that are reflected in ILO standards, and hence widely practised and widely acceptable, will give the manager a head start should he ever have to come to grips with a redundancy problem.

Above and beyond the immediate or future practical value that it can afford, the general social orientation that can be gained by a knowledge of ILO standards would appear to be an important asset for a well-rounded manager. Thus, it is hoped that this guide can also contribute in a more general way to the overall development of managers at all levels.

For these reasons, this guide should also be of considerable interest to management development institutions, in particular to those that are anxious to further the capacity of managers to understand and handle correctly the labour and social aspects of their enterprise.

However, this volume is in no way intended to be a technical or detailed treatment of international labour standards – Conventions and Recommendations of the International Labour Organisation – but rather a guide to a small selection of those ILO instruments which can have a more or less direct relevance to the day-to-day work of managers. With this end in view, and to make the significant provisions of the standards concerned more under-standable to a wide audience, certain liberties have been taken in reformulating and, in some cases, simplifying the ideas and concepts involved. We hope that this has been accomplished without distorting the meaning of the various standards or their interpretation by the competent ILO bodies. Moreover, in order not to burden the reader with interesting but non-essential details, a selection and condensation has been made of provisions within many of the instruments discussed. We have also sought, wherever relevant, to sketch the background and practices surrounding the various operative provisions and to elaborate from time to time on the significance and possible utility of certain provisions for managers where this is not apparent from a bare reading of the text.

In sum, this guide should not be used or regarded as an authoritative text on individual international labour standards but as a work of ready reference for the practising manager and management trainer or consultant.

The book begins with a discussion of the genesis and development of the International Labour Organisation and of international labour standards. It then, in three chapters dealing with the manager and trade unions, discusses successively freedom of association, the right of trade unions to organise, and collective bargaining. A chapter on consultation and communications within the enterprises highlights a number of ILO norms and guide-lines of particular interest in establishing communications policies and making them work. The guide then examines ILO standards concerning general conditions of employment and in particular wages, hours and related conditions. A chapter on physical conditions of work discusses safety and health at the workplace, including newer issues touching on quality of working life. A final chapter treats ILO standards affecting specific areas of the personnel function in the enterprise: the employment process, grievances, termination of employ-ment, wage administration and, more generally, the development of human resources.

The book was written by Alan Gladstone, Director of the ILO Indus-trial Relations and Labour Administration Department, and Secretary General of the International Industrial Relations Association. The author received, and wishes to acknowledge, substantial help from Rose-Marie Greve and Bert

Essenberg. Many colleagues in the ILO, in the Management Development Branch and the International Labour Standards Department in particular, made useful comments and suggestions and helped to improve the text.

It is hoped that the volume above all will provide managers with practical guidance and contribute, directly or indirectly, to the solution of labour problems at the workplace and enterprise.

ILO Management Development Branch
Geneva, July 1986

Chapter 1

The International Labour Organisation: its origins and history

The International Labour Organisation is one of the specialised agencies of the United Nations, but it differs from the other specialised agencies both in history and in structure: it is the only organisation in which not only governments but also employers' and workers' organisations are represented; and it was established in 1919, long before the establishment of the United Nations system. In this chapter we will briefly discuss the origins of the Organisation, the period from the establishment of the Organisation until 1944, developments after 1944 and, finally, the functions of the International Labour Office.

Various persons and groups contributed to the germination of the idea of an international labour organisation. In the first decades of the Industrial Revolution in Europe there was very little that the workers themselves could do to improve their working and living conditions. In many countries individual philanthropic manufacturers, clergymen, educators and legislators argued that family life and human dignity should come before profits, but the threat of international competition to national economies was seen by many as an obstacle to the establishment and development of protective and progressive labour legislation in view of the additional cost that such legislation would impose on employers. It was suggested in some quarters that the way out of the difficulty was to ensure that employers in all countries would face the same cost obligations by establishing minimum living and working conditions throughout the world.

Both Robert Owen (a British manufacturer and philosopher, 1771-1858) and Daniel Le Grand (a French manufactuer, 1783-1859) advocated action by governments to protect the interests of the workers, and from 1840 to 1853 Le Grand appealed to various European governments for joint agreement on labour legislation as a means of eliminating merciless competition.

Another impetus to international action on labour matters came about in the second half of the nineteenth century, which saw several attempts to form international organisations of workers and a growing feeling of international solidarity among the working class. The short-lived First International (1864-72) was soon followed by the establishment of the Second International in 1889. It was a political organisation but, in the absence of international trade union organisations, it discussed many subjects which now would be classified as primarily industrial, such as the problem of achieving the eight-hour day. Somewhat later, the first international trade secretariats and the International Federation of Trade Unions (IFTU) were established.

A significant event in this context was the establishment in 1900 of the International Association for Labour Legislation. The basic idea behind the Association was the belief that, though governments opposed the idea of inter-governmental organisations in the labour field, they might support private non-governmental organisations. The Association was based in Basle where the Swiss Government provided facilities. An "International Labour Office" was set up, directed by a bureau representing national sections. In 1906 the Association organised a diplomatic conference which adopted two draft Conventions, on the prohibition of the use of white phosphorus in the manufacture of matches and on the prohibition of night work of women. For the first time, the principle of international agreement for the regulation of labour conditions had been countenanced by a number of industrial States.

As the First World War drew towards its end, various groups started preparations for the Peace Conference. Representatives of the workers in Allied countries demanded that labour should be represented at the conference.

One of the first acts of the Peace Conference, which met in 1919, was to appoint a commission to consider the international means necessary to ensure common action on matters affecting conditions of employment, and to make recommendations concerning the form of a permanent agency to be set up for the purpose under the League of Nations. The report drafted by the commission, which met under the chairmanship of the American trade union leader Samuel Gompers, gave rise to Part XIII of the Treaty of Versailles establishing the International Labour Organisation (ILO). The First Session of the International Labour Conference (the General Conference of the ILO) was held in October 1919.

In structure the Organisation is simple. It consists of an International Labour Conference, a Governing Body and an International Labour Office. The Conference is the supreme policy-making and legislative organ; the Governing Body is the executive council; and the Office the secretariat, operational headquarters and research and information centre. The most original innovation is the tripartite character of the Organisation. Employers' and workers' representatives, equal in status with government representatives except in financial matters, sit side by side with them in the Conference and the Governing Body. In fact, the Conference is composed of four representatives of each member State, of whom two are Government delegates and two are delegates representing respectively the employers and the workers of the member State concerned. The Employers' and Workers' delegates are appointed by the governments of their countries in agreement with the most representative industrial organisations of employers and workers in the countries concerned.

In addition to the tripartite principle first described, a second tenet of the ILO is its universality. The 42 original Members of the Organisation (who were also the original Members of the League of Nations) grew to over 150 in 1984.

The year 1944 was an important one in the history of the Organisation. In that year the International Labour Conference met in Philadelphia and adopted the "Declaration of Philadelphia" and incorporated it in the ILO Constitution. The Declaration laid down two basic principles: first, that it must be the central aim of national and international policy to achieve conditions in which all men and women can pursue their material well-being and their spiritual development in freedom and dignity, economic security, and equal opportunity; and second, that all national and international efforts should be judged in the light of whether or not they help to further this aim. The Declaration can be said to have reformulated the ILO's original mandate in more comprehensive and positive terms.

In 1946 the International Labour Conference and the General Assembly of the United Nations approved the agreement negotiated between the two organisations and the ILO thus became the first specialised agency in the United Nations system.

After 1942, when the ILO reached an all-time low in membership, membership grew rapidly, particularly in the 1950s and 1960s as nearly all the countries which attained independence were admitted.

The International Labour Office – i.e. the secretariat – is headed by a Director-General appointed by the Governing Body. The functions of the Office can be divided into four main parts: (i) to act as the secretariat for the Conference, the Governing Body and other conferences and meetings; (ii) to prepare first drafts of international labour standards and promote the effective application of standards adopted; (iii) to assemble and disseminate information, and to undertake research and publish the results; and (iv) to implement operational programmes and carry out technical co-operation projects.

In the next chapter some elements of the standard-setting process of the Organisation will be discussed.

.

Chapter 2

The International Labour Code

An important part of the work of the Office is related to the preparation and supervision of the implementation of international labour standards. In his report to the 1984 session of the International Labour Conference, the Director-General said: "The development of international labour standards was the principal purpose behind the creation of the International Labour Organisation".

The term "International Labour Code" is used to denote the whole body of Conventions and Recommendations adopted by the Conference since 1919. By early 1985 the Code consisted of no fewer than 159 Conventions and 169 Recommendations covering an enormous range of subjects in the labour and social fields (a list of them, other than a few that have been superseded or were purely transitional, is to be found in the appendix).

The contents of Conventions and Recommendations which are of direct relevance to managers will be analysed in the following chapters of this guide. In this chapter the nature and effect of Conventions and Recommendations will be explained, as well as how the ILO's standard-setting machinery and procedures work. The role and responsibilities of employers and their organisations in the standard-setting process and the supervisory machinery for the application of standards will also be considered.

Conventions and Recommendations

International instruments can be divided into Conventions and Recommendations between which there exists a fundamental juridical difference. International labour Conventions are instruments explicitly designed to create obligations, while Recommendations serve to define non-obligatory norms. In other words, through their ratification, Conventions become binding on the countries that ratify them, like international treaties, while Recommendations essentially have the objective of orienting national action. They may stand alone or supplement Conventions. However, although Conventions are meant to create obligations, they have no binding force in themselves. The member States only assume the obligation to apply the provisions of Conventions which they ratify.

The standard-setting process

Government, employers, trade unions, or the Office, may come up with an idea that could constitute the germ for a Convention or Recommendation. In case such an idea evokes the interest of the Governing Body, it may be selected for inclusion in the agenda of the International Labour Conference. The first step is that the Governing Body requests the Office to prepare a preliminary brief on the law and practices of member States relating to the subject.

On the basis of this report the Governing Body decides whether or not to continue with the standard-setting process. If the Governing Body decides to place the item on the Conference agenda, a more detailed law-and-practice report and the outline of a possible instrument in questionnaire form are prepared. On the basis of the government replies, the Office prepares a set of proposed conclusions which is tantamount to an initial draft of the proposed text. When the Conference meets, it normally appoints a tripartite committee to examine the proposals and formulate conclusions. The Committee text is then submitted to the full Conference, which decides whether to include the question on the agenda of the next Conference session, with a view to the adoption, at that time, of a proposed Convention and/or Recommendation.

If the result of this first Conference discussion is positive, the Office drafts a provisional text of the proposed instrument, and sends it to the governments for comments. The Office then prepares a final report reflecting those comments and containing a revised proposed text. At the Conference, the draft is again discussed by a tripartite committee and an agreed text, often the result of long negotiations between government, employers' and workers' representatives, is put before the full Conference for approval. If it receives the votes of two-thirds of the delegates it is formally adopted as an ILO Convention or Recommendation.

Obligations of member States

From the above procedure, it is clear that employers and workers play an important role together with the governments, the more so because in those countries which have ratified the Tripartite Consultation (International Labour Standards) Convention, 1976 (No. 144), the governments concerned are bound to tripartite consultation in replying to the Office questionnaires contained in the first report as mentioned above.

Once a Convention or Recommendation has been adopted by the Conference, governments must submit both Conventions and Recommendations "to the authority or authorities within whose competence the matter lies, for the enactment of legislation or other action". They must also report back to the ILO on the measures thay have taken in that respect and on the action taken by the "competent" authority. Since the implementation of a Convention or Recommendation frequently requires legislation, the "competent authority" will in most cases be the national parliament or legislative assembly: it is for that body to decide whether the action of the International Labour Conference should be followed up at national level.

Once the submission procedure has been completed, and the steps taken communicated to the Office, the government's immediate obligations arising out of the adoption of a new instrument by the Conference are fulfilled. The report to the Office on the action taken is regarded as an important part of the overall procedure, since it is this report that enables the ILO and its supervisory bodies to ensure that the obligation to submit new instruments to the competent authorities is respected.

Only Conventions are subject to ratification by the national authorities. Once ratified, as mentioned above, Conventions become binding international obligations.

The supervisory machinery as regards Conventions and Recommendations

Under article 19 of the ILO Constitution, the Governing Body may call on all member States to report on the position of their law and practice with regard to matters dealt with in an unratified Convention or a Recommendation, the extent to which effect has been given or is proposed to be given to its provisions and the difficulties which prevent or delay its ratification. The Governing Body each year selects a number of Conventions and Recommendations to be reviewed.

In addition to the reports on *(a)* the measures with regard to newly adopted Conventions and Recommendations, and *(b)* the position of law and practice with regard to unratified Conventions and Recommendations, governments also have to report regularly on measures taken to give effect to ratified Conventions. Article 22 of the Constitution provides that each member State shall "make an annual report to the Office on the measures which it has taken to give effect to the provisions of Conventions to which it is a party ...". Because of the increasing number both of member States and of ratified Conventions, it became necessary to change the periodicity of reporting. Under the present system, detailed reports are requested every two years for certain particularly important Conventions, such as those dealing with basic human rights, while for other Conventions reports are normally requested at four-yearly intervals.

The Committee of Experts

A very important role in the supervision procedure is played by the Committee of Experts on the Application of Conventions and Recommendations. Since 1927, the examination of government reports has been carried out in the first instance by this Committee, which consists of 20 independent persons with eminent qualifications in the legal or social fields and with an intimate knowledge of labour conditions or administration, and drawn from all parts of the world. They are appointed in their personal capacity by the Governing Body for a period of three years on the proposal of the Director-General.

The functions of the Committee can be divided into three major categories: the examination of the reports on the application of ratified Conventions; the examination of reports on the situation of national law and practice with regard to selected unratified Conventions and Recommendations; and the examination of reports with regard to the submission of newly adopted Conventions and Recommendations to the competent authorities.

In examining the effect given to ratified Conventions, the Committee is not limited to the information provided by governments; it may also take into consideration the conclusions of other ILO bodies such as commissions of inquiry and the Governing Body Committee on Freedom of Association, and comments made by employers' and workers' organisations.

If the Committee finds that a government is not fully complying with the requirements of a ratified Convention, or with its obligations under the ILO Constitution regarding Conventions and Recommendations, it addresses a comment to that government, drawing attention to the shortcomings and requesting that steps be taken to eliminate them. The Committee's comments may take the form of an observation or a direct request.

To give an example of observations made by the Committee, here is a comment on the application of the Freedom of Association and Protection of the Right to Organise Convention, 1948 (No. 87):

> In its previous observation the Committee had commented on the employers' organisations which, in its opinion, do not constitute employers' organisations in the sense of the terms of the Convention, that is to say, organisations whose main purpose is to further and defend the interests of employers.

Certain observations by the Committee are sometimes directly related to the activities of employers and managers, as was the case in the following observation with regard to the Right to Organise and Collective Bargaining Convention, 1949 (No. 98):

> However, although the present legislation ensures the protection of trade union leaders and workers against dismissal for union activities, the Committee points out that no express provision protects a worker against other acts that may be harmful to him (transfer, downgrading, disciplinary measures, deprivation of or limitations on wages or social benefits, etc.) during the employment relationship or at the time of recruitment. The Committee considers that protection against acts of anti-union discrimination should be ensured by an express provision in the law. ...

The Conference committee

The report of the Committee of Experts is submitted to the International Labour Conference, where it is examined and discussed by a tripartite Conference committee on the application of Conventions and Recommendations. It is at this stage of the supervision procedure that employers' representatives play an important role.

After a general discussion, the committee examines individual cases. Governments which have been mentioned in the report of the Committee of Experts as not complying with their constitutional obligations, or not fully applying a ratified Convention, are invited to make a statement to the Conference committee to explain their position. And, although there is no formal obligation, the governments usually agree because the objective of the committee is not to apportion blame but to obtain results, i.e. better application of international labour standards.

The report of the Conference committee is submitted to the full Conference for discussion. If adopted by the Conference, the report is sent to the member States, and governments are asked to take certain points into consideration when preparing their next reports to the ILO.

Special supervisory machinery concerning freedom of association

In view of the cardinal importance of international labour standards on freedom of association, the ILO has developed special procedures for handling complaints alleging infringement of trade union rights. These procedures supplement but do not replace the regular and routine supervisory procedures.

The first special procedure involves the tripartite Governing Body Committee on Freedom of Association which examines complaints brought before it by governments, or workers' or employers' organisations and submits its findings to the Governing Body.

Another supervisory machinery in this regard is the Fact-Finding and Conciliation Commission on Freedom of Association, the members of which are independent persons appointed by the ILO Governing Body as cases arise. The procedure can be activated by the Governing Body when a complaint of infringement of trade union rights is lodged by a government, by a national employers' or workers' organisation with a direct interest in the matter, or by certain international employers' or workers' organisations. The Commission's report makes findings of fact and draws conclusions.

*   *   *

In this chapter we have discussed a very important part of the work of the Organisation. First, we have outlined the process of drafting and adopting international instruments in the form of Conventions and Recommendations destined to guide the activities of governments, employers and workers in the social and labour field. Secondly, we have discussed the machinery created for the effective supervision of the application of international labour standards.

The importance of selected Conventions and Recommendations to managers, and in particular the advantages they may offer to managers for a creative approach to fulfilling managerial responsibilities, will be discussed in the following chapters.

Chapter 3

Freedom of association

The ILO Freedom of Association and Protection of the Right to Organise Convention, 1948 (No. 87), is basically, although not exclusively, addressed to the public authorities. It seeks to provide certain guarantees to workers as well as to employers to freely associate into organisations of their own choosing. While this might seem to be a matter between the organisations and their governments, there are none the less substantial implications for managers. These implications are several. First, and perhaps foremost, the adoption of the Convention reflected a universal consensus by the world community on the principle of freedom of association for the parties to the labour-management relationship. More immediately, it endorsed and proclaimed the idea that workers can form trade unions to act collectively on their behalf in relation to management. The ratification of this Convention at the national level further endorses the principle of freedom of association and more directly contributes to the climate in which labour-management relations are to be conducted. Staff and line management at all levels cannot be insensitive to this climate, which influences the "rules of the game" under which they operate. While other standards, discussed below, might have a more immediate impact on labour relationships in the enterprise and at the workplace, managers – and employers generally – will not wish to disregard the labour-management relations climate resulting from national policy decisions. In fact managers, as we shall see, will wish to take advantage of the possibilities offered to them by interaction with trade unions for a creative approach to fulfilling managerial responsibilities. But more of this later on.

The second major implication for managers of freedom of association, quite independently of what has been discussed above, involves the possibilities of managers to profit from the communion of thought, policies and action inherent in the right of employers themselves to associate to protect and advance their interests. Thus through joint efforts management can draw upon their collective expertise in approaching managerial decision-making generally, and in the personnel and labour relations fields in particular.

A third implication of freedom of association – here again freedom of association of employers – is at the same time a constraining and a supportive one. For when managers – or employers – associate for common decision-making, a result is a situation where, given a minimum of associational discipline, managers may have to abide by certain common rules or directives emanating from their association. In other words, managers in associating together may have to give up some of their decision-making power to the larger

employers' organisation of which they are members. However, this constraint
may be more apparent than real. It may be presumed that longer-range benefits
of association will result. These would include in particular a stronger position
in relation to the government and the trade union movement and the advantage
of common services such as those in support of collective bargaining or dispute
adjustment. But common decision-making at a level above that of the enterprise or the particular sphere of action of the manager concerned can also
insulate that manager from being held responsible for action that might have to
be taken in the personnel and labour relations fields where the relevant
decisions are taken on behalf of the member enterprises of an employers'
association. Moreover whatever constraints may come about as a result of
associative policy-making or decision-taking, it must be recognised that those
decisions or policies are normally based on democratic procedures in which the
manager or employer or his representative will have participated.

To return now to freedom of association for workers, i.e. the exercise
of trade union rights, a few additional points of significance to managers might
be stressed.

The records of the bodies that supervise the application of Convention
No. 87 is replete with cases in which governments have sought to deny trade
union rights guaranteed under the Convention. Some of these cases are of
rather direct interest for managers.

Trade union multiplicity

A case in point is that of "breakaway" and multiple unionism. Managers are not unaware of the considerable advantages, if dealings are to be had
with unions, of dealing with a single union body – at least in respect of particular groups of workers, but even more generally in respect of all or the bulk of
the workers in an enterprise. Indeed trade unions themselves recognise that "in
unity there is strength". However, the application of that principle can run
counter to the perhaps more limited and special interests of smaller groupings
of workers formed into unions reflecting political, ideological, religious or other
divisions, or even differences based upon leadership personalities and aspir-
ations. Thus governments in certain cases, whether motivated by a desire to
strengthen the trade union movement or to avoid threats to the proper
functioning of the national economy, have attempted to impose trade union
unity on workers. The supervisory organs of the ILO, even while recognising
the arguments in favour of the desirability of avoiding proliferation of overlap-
ping trade union groupings, have insisted that efforts to impose trade union
unity through official action by the State would run counter to the principles of
Convention No. 87, in particular those concerning the right of workers to establish and join organisations of their own choosing. Trade union diversity was
clearly not intended to be an obligation, but the Convention requires that this
diversity be a possibility.

It is important for managers to understand that in spite of the dictate of the Convention forbidding governments to impose trade union unity, it is not necessarily incompatible with the Convention for laws or regulations to provide for the designation of a single trade union, that is most representative of the workers concerned, as the exclusive bargaining agent for those workers. In such cases, however, the determination of the exclusive representative must be surrounded by certain safeguards and, in particular, that the determination is made on the basis of objective criteria (such as majority support by the workers concerned), and that the determination be for a fixed period. Not infrequently the determination is made by an impartial, independent body.

This is of great importance for managers who may find it not only bothersome and inefficient to deal with a number of unions. Moreover trade union multiplicity can present a serious threat to the very well-being of the enterprise. In many cases the obligation to bargain or otherwise deal with a number of unions, particularly with regard to the same category of workers, will result in differing demands, "leapfrogging" by the competing unions, dissension, divisiveness and friction among the workers, and the danger of disputes and stoppages by various groups for reasons that can be traced to relations between the unions concerned rather than relations with management. This being said, it should be remembered that Convention No. 87 is principally directed at state action and policies. Thus the context in which the manager finds himself with duties and obligations vis-à-vis trade unions (multiplicity, exclusive representation, etc.) is one which may be state established and his policies will be formulated within the rules of the game (if any) laid down by the State.

Union security and the check-off

Another question is that of union security arrangements, that is, the various forms of compulsory trade union membership. These arrangements may require that an enterprise can only engage workers who are union members, or members of a given union; or that non-members may be engaged, but upon engagement must become union members. Such arrangements are usually made by agreement between the parties to collective bargaining. It is thus helpful for managers to understand the issues involved as well as the position of ILO standards on the matter. Convention No. 87 has been interpreted as neither authorising nor prohibiting voluntary union security arrangements. In the words of the Freedom of Association Committee of the ILO, "... those countries – and more particularly those countries having trade union pluralism – would in no way be bound ... to permit union security clauses either by law or as a matter of custom, while other countries which allow such clauses would not be placed in the position of being unable to ratify the Convention." [1]

Related to the question of union security is that of arrangements for withholding members' union dues and contributions at the source by the employer and their remittance to the union, that is, the "check-off". Such arrangements of course impose an obligation on management, usually voluntarily acquiesced in through agreement with the union. They can also involve a fair degree of bookkeeping and accounting work for management. While national practices – and legislation – differ, the Convention itself could not be invoked to call into question agreed arrangements, as such.

As has been seen, ILO standards neither encourage nor prohibit voluntary union security or check-off arrangements. Indeed, varying national practices, in no way inconsistent with Convention No. 87, can be found in which union security arrangements – or certain types thereof – are permitted or prohibited. (In many countries the law and regulations are silent on this point.) For instance, in certain countries a requirement of pre-engagement membership is prohibited, but arrangements agreed between unions and management regarding post-engagement compulsory membership are valid (and even enforceable). It should be added that the ILO supervisory bodies have held that where union security arrangements are in force, there might be unfair discrimination if unreasonable conditions made it impossible or difficult for workers to become members in the union concerned. The ILO supervisory bodies have also held that when the *law* imposes union security – either by making union membership compulsory or by making union contributions payable in such circumstances as to amount to the same thing – this requirement could be incompatible with the principles of Convention No. 87.

Managers of course must be aware of the situation regarding national law and practice in relation to union security if they are to entertain constructive relations with trade unions, but it is also helpful for them to place national law and practice in the perspective of international standards.

Public sector, supervisory and other special categories

There are two additional aspects of Convention No. 87 that are of interest to managers. These concern the coverage of the Convention. For managers in the public sector or services, it should be noted that Convention No. 87 does not exclude even civil servants and officials in the public service, and much less workers in public sector industrial, commercial and other enterprises. Just as in the case of other workers, any prohibition of the right to association of workers in the service of the State would be incompatible with the principle of the Convention that workers, *without distinction whatsoever*, have the right to establish organisations of their own choosing without previous authorisation.

Managers will also be interested by the situation of supervisory employees with regard to Convention No. 87. Here the ILO supervisory bodies have been somewhat more circumspect in their pronouncements. It appears that national laws or regulations prohibiting supervisory employees from joining *workers'* organisations could be countenanced provided that the term "supervisors" is limited to employees who genuinely represent the interests of employers. In other words the definition of "supervisor" is one that must be strictly drawn if the exclusion of this group from its coverage is to be in conformity with the Convention. In practice there are countries where supervisory employees are members of unions along with non-supervisory workers and countries which prohibit such membership. Many in the latter group do, however, permit supervisory employees to form their own distinct organisations.

In passing it might be mentioned that the only general categories which, under its terms, can be excluded from the benefits and protection of Convention No. 87 are the armed forces and the police.

Trade union leadership, "outsiders" and political activities

The Convention also protects the right of workers and their organisations to elect freely their leaders. In many countries there has been substantial discussion of the role of "outsiders" as trade union leaders. Managers in particular have not infrequently voiced concern about having to treat with union representatives who were neither from the enterprise nor, at times, even from the industry. These concerns are not unrelated to abuses that are reported from time to time whereby outsiders – perhaps politicians, perhaps those seeking only monetary gain – use trade unions for their own selfish purposes and not to further the interest of the members or the workers in general. Such leadership, where it is in evidence, can obviously present difficulties for effective and constructive labour relations and hence for good management. However, these fears and concerns sometimes neglect the fact that effective leadership of trade unions cannot always be found among the workers themselves in the enterprise or industry.

In any event Convention No. 87 has been interpreted in a manner so that blanket restrictions on outsiders serving as union officers or officials may not be countenanced. For example, national legislation that would provide that all trade union leaders must belong to the occupation in which the union functions would undoubtedly raise problems of conformity with the Convention. Likewise provisions requiring trade union leaders, at the time of their election, to have been engaged in the particular occupation or trade for more than a year would not be in harmony with the Convention.

As regards political activities of trade unions, it is interesting to note that the Committee on Freedom of Association of the Governing Body of the ILO has implicity recognised that nothing would prevent unions, in accordance with the will of their members, from establishing relations with a political party or from other forms of legal political action in pursuance of the union's economic and social objectives. In fact, a general prohibition on political activities for unions could raise difficulties of conformity with Convention No. 87.

* * *

The freedom of association discussion has focused thus far on matters concerning relations between workers' (and, incidentally, employers') organisations and the public authorities – which is indeed the focus of Convention No. 87. We have seen nevertheless that these relations contribute mightily to the framework within which labour relations are conducted between trade unions and management. Within this discussion we have also raised, although in passing, the implications for managers of the application of the protection, provisions and requirements of Convention No. 87 in respect of employers and their organisations, again chiefly in the context of their relations with the public authorities. In the next chapter we shall focus more on the requirements of international labour standards in the more direct relations between workers and their organisations on the one hand, and employers and their organisations on the other. First and foremost in this regard is the general principle that where governments ensure that the right to associate is guaranteed by appropriate measures, for that guarantee to be effective there must be further measures to protect the workers against anti-union discrimination in respect of their employment and to ensure that workers' organisations are not subject to interference in their affairs by employers.

Note

[1] ILO: *Freedom of association*, Digest of decisions and principles of the Committee on Freedom of Association of the Governing Body of the ILO (Geneva, 3rd ed., 1985), pp. 52-53.

Chapter 4

The right to organise

Convention No. 98 – the Right to Organise and Collective Bargaining Convention, 1949 – addresses itself to relations between workers and management (although imposing obligations on governments to ensure that certain principles are adhered to in those bilateral relations), whereas, as is evident from the previous discussion, Convention No. 87 essentially addresses itself to relations between the State and the parties to the labour-management relationship.

Thus we are now very much at the manager's level. For the manager, directly or through his enterprise's employers' association, will be faced with situations where workers in his enterprise seek to join or establish trade unions and, through such unions, seek to interact with the manager. What is to be his position or attitude in the face of initiatives of this kind by his workers and their trade unions?

Anti-union discrimination

The thrust of Convention No. 98 is to ensure that the interaction can take place in an arms-length fashion and with a reasonable degree of autonomy of the parties. As a first step workers are to be protected from management action which could prejudice their right to join or establish trade unions or, more broadly, protected against acts of anti-union discrimination in their employment. This means that workers' employment cannot be made subject to their not joining a trade union, or to giving up their membership. It also means that workers are protected against acts of discrimination by management (dismissal, demotion, discriminatory transfers or other prejudicial action) because of union membership or activity. This protection is viewed as particularly important as regards trade union officers and also in terms of ensuring that workers' organisations have the right to elect their representatives in full freedom, as prescribed by Convention No. 87 discussed above.

Convention No. 98 provides, as regards union activities, that this protection extends to such activities outside working hours. Where the activities are within working hours, the consent of the employer may be required. It is thus clear that the protection is neither complete nor unconditional. For example, trade unionists who might take time off from work, even to attend workers' education courses, without permission from the management, would not necessarily, on this basis alone, be protected against disciplinary action.

In many countries, however, which in line with Convention No. 98 have established some sort of appeals procedures (through the courts or other bodies) or other machinery for ensuring the required protection, care has normally been taken to try to ascertain the real reasons for action taken against workers where anti-union discrimination is alleged. Moreover, at times, the severity and consistency of sanctions will be examined to ensure that more stringent sanctions are not invoked in the event of a union involvement in the alleged disciplinary breach. In this regard, the ILO Governing Body Committee on Freedom of Association found it difficult in a particular case to accept as a coincidence unrelated to trade union activity that, immediately after a strike, disciplinary boards were convened which, ostensibly on the basis of their service records, ordered the dismissal of a number of strikers including the seven members of the union committee. It should, however, be emphasised again, and this is of key importance for managers, that the Committee has stated repeatedly that the fact that a worker holds a trade union office does not confer upon him unconditional immunity from disciplinary action or dismissal in any circumstances. Notwithstanding, the Committee has commented favourably on provisions which would place on the employer the burden of proving that such action was justified and did not constitute an anti-union discriminatory measure. Indeed, the Committee saw this as one of the means to ensure effective protection against such discrimination. In view of these requirements, and as a matter of enlightened personnel policy, it may be suggested that managers consider the utility of drafting a clear policy statement in this regard which might be accompanied by specific instructions to managers at all levels.

Management support of trade unions and provision of facilities

A manager may also be faced with a request from a trade union for certain assistance to facilitate the union's functioning – or perhaps to ensure its very existence. At times managers on their own initiative may wish to provide assistance to unions. In this area, managers will wish to exercise a certain degree of caution. In fact the framers of Convention No. 98 sought to ensure the independence of trade unions from management control, domination or influence by forbidding acts of interference by either party in the other's establishment, functioning or administration. The Convention cites as interference those acts designed to promote the establishment of unions under employer domination, or financial or other support for unions, the object of which is to place the union under employer control. These strictures are of course aimed at promoting a system of labour-management relations where the two parties are independent and can engage in genuine mutual dealings in the best interest of their constituents.

In interpreting Convention No. 98, the ILO supervisory bodies have referred to practices which could run afoul of the provisions on "interference", even without there being an intention of domination or control of the union by the employer. For example, it has been found that requesting employees to state to which trade union they belonged, even where such request was not intended to interfere with the exercise of trade union rights, could be regarded as such interference. Thus it behoves managers to weigh carefully actions which they might envisage taking where implications might be drawn regarding the impact of such action on trade unions and workers' organisational rights.

However, Convention No. 98 cannot and should not be read as negating the possibility of any and all action by managers to facilitate the task of trade unions. Indeed, the Workers' Representatives Convention, 1971 (No. 135), and Recommendation, 1971 (No. 143), specifically call for the provision of certain facilities to trade union representatives (as well as other workers' representatives). The Convention calls for the provision to union representatives of such facilities in the enterprise as may be appropriate in order to enable them to carry out their representative functions promptly and efficiently. But the Convention does not provide the basis for unlimited or unreasonable demands for facilities, for it stipulates that the granting of such facilities is not to impair the efficient operation of the enterprise. Further, in affording facilities, account is to be taken of the needs, size and capabilities of the enterprise and of the industrial relations system of the country concerned.

Recommendation No. 143 supplements Convention No. 135 by specifying the types of facilities to be made available or countenanced by management. Time off without loss in pay or other benefits, as necessary to carry out their representation functions in the enterprise, is called for. Reasonable time limits may be set on the amount of time off and, in the absence of standing provisions, the representatives may be required to obtain permission (which permission is not to be unreasonably withheld).

Other facilities related to the person of the representative relate to granting representatives access, as necessary for them to carry out their functions, to various workplaces in the enterprise, and access to management representatives with decision-making power. The Recommendation also calls for the granting of time off to workers' representatives as necessary for attending training courses, trade union and other types of meetings which will enable representatives to carry out their functions effectively. It is left open as to whether or not such time off should be paid by the employer.

The provision of these personal facilities is not aimed at giving the trade union or other workers' representative a privileged position. It is rather a question of providing the possibilities for the establishment of an effective system of labour relations at the enterprise level. Moreover, the various caveats and reservations – "to enable them to carry out their functions"; taking account of the "needs, size and capabilities" of the enterprise; not impairing the "efficient operation" of the enterprise; "reasonable limits", "as may be necessary" – are designed to avoid abuses as regards the granting or utilisation of facilities for the union and other representatives.

The Workers' Representatives Recommendation goes on to provide for additional facilities which perhaps deal more with functions than attributes relating to the person of the representative. These include the possibility of trade union representatives collecting union dues on the premises, posting trade union notices (in agreed places) and distributing union documents (relating to normal trade union activities) in the enterprise. Finally, the Recommendation provides for the possibility of management making available to workers' representatives material facilities and information needed in their functions as well as for the possibility of access to the enterprise, under certain conditions, of outside representatives of trade unions having members in the enterprise.

This last group of facilities, which largely concern certain activities of union (and other workers') representatives, also seeks to avoid possible abuses through references to arrangements "agreed with the management", not prejudicing "the orderly operation" of the enterprise, "necessary for the exercise of their functions", reference to implementation "consistent with national practice", etc.

But above and beyond the reservations and caveats, there are positive reasons for managers to take an interest in the provision of facilities. It may be recalled and repeated that, as is the case with many ILO international instruments, Convention No. 135 and Recommendation No. 143 were the product of negotiations and compromises between worker and employer delegates to the International Labour Conference. They represent not only a set of ideas with which the parties thought that they could live but, of more significance, ideas that if properly put into practice would work to the advantage of all by enhancing the climate of constructive relations within the enterprise. For a union to be in place in the enterprise and be either ineffectual owing to restrictions in time or place of its representative's movements, or for such representatives to be untrained or insufficiently trained, or unable to communicate adequately with the workers they represent, or otherwise be unable to carry out in a reasonable manner their mandate, can only lead to frustration and bitterness which in turn can adversely affect the operation of the enterprise – its stability of labour relations and general climate, its productivity and, hence the "bottom line".

In 1978, the International Labour Conference, recognising that Convention No. 98 and related instruments did not cover certain categories of public servants, adopted the Labour Relations (Public Service) Convention (No. 151). Similar to Convention No. 98, this Convention provides protection for public servants as regards their right to join and retain membership and engage in activities of public service employee organisations, and provides against interference by public authorities in the establishment, functioning or administration of public employees' organisations. Moreover, in a manner analogous to the provisions of the Workers' Representatives Convention, 1971 (No. 135), the Labour Relations (Public Service) Convention, 1978 (No. 151), and its companion Recommendation, 1978 (No. 159), provide, but with far less specificity, for affording facilities to representatives of public employees' organisations so that they can carry out their functions; the granting of such facilities should, however, not impair the efficient operation of the administration or service.

Chapter 5

Collective bargaining

Collective bargaining – or the negotiation between trade unions and employers or their associations of terms and conditions of employment and related procedural matters – is generally recognised as the keystone of organised labour-management relations. Negotiations between trade unions and employers are considered in most industrial relations systems to be the very *raison d'être* of trade unionism – the chief means for protecting and advancing the interests of the workers. Indeed, much of what has been discussed above regarding freedom of association, non-discrimination and protection and facilities for workers' representatives has as its purpose the facilitating of collective bargaining. But collective bargaining is not necessarily a one-way street involving trade union demands followed by management reaction. It can be a creative device utilisable by the parties both to solve problems and initiate new and innovative ideas. This implies that negotiations need not be a matter of table-thumping and unreasoned and unreasonable demands by one or the other party (although some emotion may have a rightful place in the process), but a constructive dialogue leading to mutually beneficial compromises.

The "right" of collective bargaining was recognised even before its legislative consecration under the Right to Organise and Collective Bargaining Convention, 1949 (No. 98). As mentioned earlier, in 1944 the General Conference, at its historic session in Philadelphia, adopted a declaration known by the name of that city and forming an annex to the ILO Constitution. The declaration solemnly calls for the promotion of programmes which will achieve "the effective recognition of the right of collective bargaining". Convention No. 98 itself calls for measures appropriate to national conditions to be taken, "... to encourage and promote the full development and utilisation of voluntary negotiation between employers or employers' organisations and workers' organisations, with a view to the regulation of terms and conditions of employment by means of collective agreements".

It is important to understand, particularly since it is not entirely clear from the language of the Convention and of Recommendation No. 91 concerning collective agreements, that the right to bargain collectively has been considered by the ILO supervisory bodies as an essential element in freedom of association. The Freedom of Association Committee of the ILO Governing Body has stressed the importance it attaches to good faith bargaining by both trade unions and management but has demurred to enter into ruling on considerations concerning whether one party adopts an amenable or uncompromising attitude towards the demands of the other party.

Public sector and public services

The question may well arise, particularly for managers in the public sector or in public services, as to the collective bargaining rights of public servants or other workers in the public sector. Convention No. 98 itself provides that it does not deal with the position of public servants "engaged in the administration of the State", but that it is not to be construed as prejudicing their rights or status in any way. Thus there is a possibility of exclusion of such workers from collective bargaining rights under Convention No. 98, although more modern practice has tended rather to the extension of bargaining rights to such employees.

But the important point to bear in mind is that the possible exclusion is limited to those engaged in the administration of the State. Thus managers in the public sector should be aware that bargaining rights are guaranteed to workers in public industrial or commercial enterprises and nationalised enterprises. The dividing line between such groups and those engaged in the administration of the State may not always be crystal clear, but the ILO Committee of Experts on the Application of Conventions and Recommendations has pointed out that it would be contrary to Convention No. 98 to exclude from its scope persons employed by the State who do not act as agents of the public authority (regardless of their status or what they may be called).

The basic distinction would seem to be between civil servants in government departments or comparable bodies and others who may be employed by public or para-statal undertakings. On this basis – and by way of example – staff of a national radio and television organisation, administrative staff of a national university, employees in the postal and telecommunications services and civil aviation technicians (even working under the jurisdiction of the armed forces) have all been found to be within the scope of Convention No. 98 under which they are to enjoy collective bargaining rights.

The Labour Relations (Public Service) Convention, 1978 (No. 151), and Recommendation, 1978 (No. 159), do modify the situation as reflected by Convention No. 98, in that the Convention provides for the encouragement and promotion of machinery for *negotiation* of terms and conditions of employment between the public authorities and public employees' organisations, "or of such other methods as will allow representatives of public employees to participate in the determination of these matters". Managers in the public service may thus wish to note that, under this language, negotiation (i.e. collective bargaining) is still not *required* in the case of public employees, since provision is made for the possibility of other methods, for example effective consultation procedures and practices. It should be stressed, however, that increasingly, and in line with the thrust of the Convention, collective bargaining is accepted in the public service.

Level of bargaining and trade union recognition

There are a number of technical questions that might have to be faced by managers with regard to collective bargaining. One of these is the level of bargaining. Is bargaining to take place at the workplace level, the enterprise level, the industry level (for a region or for the whole country) or even the national level – or at some place in between those levels – or even at several levels? It will be remembered that Convention No. 98 refers to negotiations between "employers or employers' organisations" and organisations of workers. The Collective Agreements Recommendation, 1951 (No. 91), refers to agreements (the outcome of collective bargaining) regarding working conditions and terms of employment "between an employer, or a group of employers or one or more employers' organisations, on the one hand, and one or more representative workers' organisations ...".

Thus there are no provisions which would prescribe a particular level of bargaining, this being left to national practice and the will of the parties concerned. The Collective Bargaining Recommendation, 1981 (No. 163), nevertheless states that bargaining should be possible at all levels and that where bargaining takes place at several levels, there should be co-ordination as between the various levels.

There is a preliminary, although capital, question which must be dealt with before bargaining takes place, regardless of the level of bargaining. This is the question of trade union recognition for collective bargaining purposes. In a situation of trade union pluralism, recognition, particularly at enterprise level, will frequently pose dilemmas for managers who are approached by one or more unions with a view to collective bargaining. The question is perhaps less striking in cases of industry-wide bargaining and where there is often a well-established and unified trade union movement, and at which level managers are not faced with what they might consider a direct threat to their authority and prerogatives.

Where bargaining relations are centred at the enterprise level it should be understood that the relevant ILO standards in no way preclude requirements under which bargaining is limited to the single most representative union. In other words, management is not bound, and governments are not obliged to require management (at least under the relevant international standards), to negotiate with any other union claiming to speak for the workers concerned.

A note of caution should be raised. That is that only in cases where there is no representative trade union may management seek to engage in bargaining with representatives of unorganised workers. Direct negotiations between the enterprise and its employees, bypassing representative organisations where these exist, have been held to be "detrimental to the principle that negotiation between employers and organisations of workers should be encouraged and promoted".

Thus, as regards recognition of unions by management for purposes of collective bargaining, the principle of representative character is all-important.

Stated affirmatively, employers should recognise, for the purposes of collective bargaining, organisations that are representative of workers employed by them. This can involve objective verification of that representative character. While majority adherence or support for the union concerned would normally be conclusive evidence of its representative character, recognition of unions with less than majority support, in the absence of a majority union, could also be envisaged.

Procedures for recognition of representative trade unions, or determining the representative character of unions, may be based on voluntary agreement of a bipartite or tripartite nature. These are frequently concluded at the national level (particularly in the case of tripartite agreements) but many also are found at industry or even at enterprise levels. The procedures may also be based on legislation which will often compel the management to recognise and deal with (bargain with) a trade union meeting certain conditions.

In many countries there is machinery – legislatively based and/or under the aegis of the public authorities – to determine representative status through ballots or other means of testing the preferences of the workers concerned. The Collective Bargaining Recommendation, 1981, does state, with regard to official recognition procedures for bargaining purposes, that the determination should be based on pre-established objective criteria with regard to the unions' representative character and that the procedures should be established in consultation with representative employers' and workers' organisations.

Subjects and scope of collective bargaining

On the question of the subject-matter of bargaining, the supervisory bodies have never sought to sustain a right – under either Conventions No. 87 or No. 98 – to an unlimited scope for bargaining issues. Indeed, at least in so far as government or public services are concerned, the supervisory bodies have commented that there are certain matters which clearly concern the management and operation of government business and can hence reasonably be regarded as outside the scope of negotiation. They have also recognised that certain other matters are primarily or essentially related to conditions of employment and hence "bargainable". The Collective Bargaining Convention, 1981, calls for negotiations to: determine working conditions and terms of employment; regulate relations between employers and workers; and regulate relations between employers or their organisations and workers' organisations. Thus, international standards clearly include "relational" matters as well as "economic" issues as appropriate for bargaining. Such relationship matters could encompass agreement on trade union representation at the workplace, grievance and dispute adjustment procedures (including no-strike and no-lockout provisions), disciplinary rules, redundancy procedures, and a host of other matters limited only by the imagination and interests of unions and management.

The difficulty concerning the subject-matter of bargaining arises with regard to distinguishing between those matters which are considered appropriate matters for bargaining and those which may not be so considered. Often this problem turns on the question of managerial rights or prerogatives. It may be noted, however, that in the practice of many countries the scope and ambit of those rights or prerogatives are dynamic and in a state of almost permanent flux. It is frequently through judicial decision in some countries, and overriding procedural agreements (sometimes at the national level) in others, that the boundaries of negotiable and non-negotiable items are set. But this is rarely done in a manner that would render these boundaries static. Both changing views of "appropriateness" and the emergence of new and sometimes dramatically different issues (for example, those relating to new technology or new organisational ideas) call for frequent reappraisal and re-evaluation in the area of bargainable and non-bargainable subjects. Furthermore, in many industrial relations systems, the ever-present theme of relative bargaining power and the relative strength of the parties cannot be easily ignored in regulating questions of which issues are bargainable.

Authority and information

Another point of particular importance to managers, and one stressed in the Collective Bargaining Recommendation, 1981, is that the bargainers should have the requisite authority to commit their sides. While this would not preclude, particularly in the case of unions, consultations within their respective organisations, it should be recognised that few things are as prejudicial to effective bargaining, and a proper climate for bargaining, as the inability of the spokesman of one or the other party to take a reasonably firm decision on the issues in contention. Thus managers involved in collective bargaining should be those with appropriate status and responsibility so as to be able to commit the employer or employers' association concerned.

A further impediment to effective bargaining would be insufficient information. It is not unusual for management to be hesitant in providing information of various types to the union with which it is negotiating. However, if we agree that effective bargaining is a key to sound labour relations desired by all parties, managers should be willing to provide to the union the information necessary for bargaining. On this point, the Collective Bargaining Recommendation cites the need for access to information if one is to have meaningful negotiations. It specifically provides that management, at the request of the union, should make available information on the economic and social situation of the enterprise as necessary for meaningful negotiations. But the Recommendation also recognises that public disclosure of certain information might prejudice the operation of the enterprise. Thus it provides that information may be given under an engagement to keep the information confidential.

The right to strike and collective bargaining

While strikes may be a tool used by trade unions for attaining varied objectives – e.g. organisation or recognition, correcting alleged unfair treatment, redress of grievances, even political objectives – a most common resort to strikes is had where there is a breakdown or deadlock in collective bargaining (and perhaps in a situation where statutory or other dispute resolution procedures such as conciliation, mediation and fact-finding have been exhausted). In industrial relations practice as it has evolved or been adopted in many countries, strikes are a measure of last resort. Moreover, for certain of the situations referred to above, special machinery has been set up in order to obviate any need for recourse to strikes. Thus in many countries disputes as to trade union recognition, alleged discriminatory practices or those concerning questions of the application of existing collective agreements are subject to special procedures (through administrative labour boards, arbitration bodies or labour courts, for example) to the exclusion of recourse to direct industrial action such as strikes.

It is interesting to note that there is only one direct reference to strikes (and lock-outs) in ILO standards. This is found in the Voluntary Conciliation and Arbitration Recommendation, 1951 (No. 92), which merely states that, where disputes have been submitted voluntarily to conciliation or arbitration procedures, the parties should be encouraged to abstain from strikes or lock-outs while conciliation or arbitration is in progress and, in the case of arbitration, to accept the arbitration award. However, the ILO supervisory bodies have made a number of pronouncements on the right to strike as an aspect of freedom of association and, more particularly, trade union rights.

It has been held that any general and absolute prohibition of the right to strike would not be in conformity with Convention No. 87 and that this right is generally recognised as a legitimate and, indeed, essential means by which workers and organisations may promote and defend their occupational or economic interests. Thus strikes of a purely political nature and those decided systematically long before collective bargaining takes place would not be protected within the scope of the principles of freedom of association. Nor would the prohibition of strikes concerning a difference in interpretation of a legal text constitute a breach of freedom of association. Restrictions on the right to strike may be countenanced in respect of essential services or in the public service, but in such cases adequate guarantees should be provided to safeguard the workers' interests, such as impartial and speedy conciliation and arbitration proceedings in which the parties concerned can fully take part.

However, it must be emphasised that all publicly owned enterprises are not excluded from the protection of the right to strike afforded under Convention No. 87. Indeed, the Committee of Experts on the Application of Conventions and Recommendations has stated that "the principle whereby the right to strike may be limited or prohibited in the public services or in essential services, whether public, semi-public or private, would become meaningless if [national] legislation defined the public service or essential services too broadly". It goes without saying, on the basis of this statement, that industrial, commercial and similar enterprises that happen to be in the public sector would normally be covered by the protection of Convention No. 87 concerning the right to strike.

Settlement of disputes: conciliation and arbitration

We have already talked about protection of the right of workers to strike. However, it is often the case in industrial relations systems that prior to, or as an alternative to, resort to strike relating to disputes arising out of deadlocks in collective bargaining, certain measures may be taken or certain procedures followed aimed at resolving the dispute without recourse to such direct action. Various ILO instruments address themselves to these possibilities.

The Voluntary Conciliation and Arbitration Recommendation, 1951, mentioned above refers in general to labour disputes without distinguishing those which arise out of an impasse in bargaining from other types of labour disputes. But there is no doubt that its provisions have a primary impact on bargaining disputes. It is of course a key point that the conciliation and arbitration procedures called for by the instrument are those to which recourse is had voluntarily – i.e. with the agreement, consent or acquiescence of the parties concerned. As mentioned earlier, the parties are expected to refrain from direct action, at least during the time that conciliation is in progress.

Conciliation, although not defined in Recommendation No. 92, refers to a process of third-party intervention (public or private) aimed at helping the parties themselves to reach agreement. The conciliator can in no way impose a settlement, and in some cases will even refrain from making recommendations. Underscoring the connection of conciliation with bargaining, the Recommendation provides that settlements arrived at through conciliation should be regarded as equivalent to collective agreements concluded in the usual manner. This in fact is a quite usual situation, particularly where conciliation is in fact an extension of collective bargaining by bringing a neutral third party into the negotiations. Just as the result of bargaining is consecrated in a collective agreement, the results of conciliation – which indeed constitutes a bargain by the very definition of conciliation – should be an agreement in every way comparable to that arrived at through exclusively bipartite bargaining.

As opposed to conciliation, arbitration refers to third party intervention in a labour dispute in which the third party – the arbitrator – takes the decision-making power out of the hands of the parties and himself dictates the terms of the settlement of the dispute. The arbitral decision is usually called an "award". Under most national practices involving arbitration, the award is binding and enforceable and the rendering of an award would preclude resort to direct action such as strikes as a means of defying or challenging the award. Recommendation No. 92 of course deals with arbitration that is voluntary, and indeed compulsory arbitration systems (i.e. those under which the parties, or one of them, are compelled, regardless of their wishes, to submit to arbitration under force of legislation or government policy) present serious problems of conformity with Convention No. 87. This is particularly so where, as is frequently the case under systems of compulsory arbitration, the requirement is accompanied by a prohibition of strikes.

The term "voluntary arbitration" denotes that the parties to a dispute have all voluntarily agreed to the procedure. It does not preclude compulsion in the sense of the binding nature and enforceability of the award. Nevertheless, the Voluntary Conciliation and Arbitration Recommendation, 1951, is careful on this point and merely states that "if a dispute has been submitted to arbitration for final settlement with the consent of all parties concerned, the latter should be encouraged to abstain from strikes and lock-outs while the arbitration is in progress and to accept the arbitration award". It adds that the Recommendation may not be interpreted as limiting the right to strike.

What, then, is the interest of managers in voluntary conciliation and arbitration? One interest is clear – avoidance of disputes leading to work stoppages. This alone would be good reason for managers to promote or welcome conciliation and arbitration procedures and even to seek to enter into voluntary arrangements with unions to this end. But effective settlement procedures can go beyond merely enhancing the possibilities of avoiding strikes and stoppages. When soundly fashioned and utilised they can contribute to a general enhancement of the climate of industrial relations in enterprises and industries since the parties, and the trade unions and their members in particular, feel that their problems will be ultimately dealt with fairly and constructively. Such arrangements are all the more attractive if the parties can rely on the expertise, judgement and professional qualities of conciliators and arbitrators.

Of course voluntary reliance on arbitration as a final step in the disputes resolution procedure (as regards disputes arising out of deadlocks in collective bargaining) should not lead to a situation where managers (or trade unions) consider that they no longer need to make a serious effort at bargaining since failure to agree will be taken care of at a later stage. Regardless of the excellence of the arbitrator, and the soundness of the presentation of their case by the parties before the arbitrator, no third-party decision can match a settlement by the parties themselves who know intimately the problems in issue as well as the temper and climate of the enterprise or industry in which the settlement will have to be carried out.

Managers may wish to consider the possibility of proposing to their union counterparts the joint adoption of a scheme, of general or limited scope, for arbitration of interest disputes arising out of a failure to agree in collective bargaining. (Conciliation may be agreed upon also but usually there are government facilities available for this purpose.) There are numerous examples of such arrangements, such as in major industries of Switzerland (metalworking and watchmaking, chemicals) and in the United States (steel production). In both cases, where forms of industry-wide collective bargaining take place (and where the parties otherwise enjoy the right to strike or lock out in pursuance of their bargaining claims and demands), the parties voluntarily eschew strikes or lock-outs and agree to submit unresolved issues to arbitration. In the United

States steel industry, this mutual engagement is coupled with a form of early or continuous bargaining during the period of the collective agreement which anticipates and tries to resolve contentious issues well prior to the expiration of the existing agreement. It is interesting to note in the case of the United States steel industry that there has been neither recourse to arbitration nor a strike since these arrangements were agreed upon some 20 years ago. In other words, agreement was reached in collective bargaining on modifications before the end of each of the successive expirations of existing agreements. Is this perhaps an indication of the constructive use to which voluntary arbitration arrangements may be put?

Managers in the public service will wish to note that the Labour Relations (Public Service) Convention, 1978 (No. 151), stressed the need, when collective bargaining reaches a deadlock, to have recourse for settlement of the dispute to independent and impartial machinery such as mediation, conciliation and arbitration. This provision is of particular significance in those cases, quite widespread, where public servants do not have the right to strike in support of their demands and claims when bargaining does not lead to agreement.

Nature of the collective agreement

Eventually, in the absence of resort to arbitration, the parties to collective bargaining, if their relationship is to continue, will reach an accord – a collective agreement. An object of that agreement is, or should be, to guarantee to the parties a certain stability in their relations, usually for a determined period. There is mutual benefit in collective agreements. Workers know that their wages and other terms and conditions of employment are assured and not subject to change at the whim of their employer; trade unions have successfully fulfilled one of their prime functions vis-à-vis their members, and have reinforced their institutional role as co-regulator with management as regards at least a significant area of decision-making; managers can rely on a degree of stability and foreseeability as to labour costs and as to the state of labour-management relations in the enterprise or industry. This is not to mention that the fact of negotiating the collective agreement can bring a degree of maturity in those relations and contribute to the establishment of a climate of mutual confidence and trust.

But, for the collective agreement to maximise the possibilities of these desirable results, certain conditions should surround its conclusion. Many of these are referred to in ILO standards.

The Collective Agreements Recommendation, 1951 (No. 91), refers to agreements "in writing". It is rather elementary, particularly from the point of view of the manager, that the rules governing conditions at the workplace should, wherever possible, be written in order to avoid confusion and contention as to what was actually agreed upon.

More significantly, perhaps, the Recommendation provides that agreements should be binding on the signatories and on those on whose behalf the agreement is concluded. It is important – and this is emphasised by the Recommendation – that individual contracts of employment cannot serve to impose conditions contrary to those of the collective agreement, although stipulations of individual contracts more favourable to the workers than those in the collective agreement would not be considered as contrary to the collective agreement. As a matter of good personnel policy, irrespective of the cited requirements of the Recommendation, it is almost inconceivable that a manager would seek to apply conditions in individual cases less favourable to the worker than those provided for in a collective agreement. To do so would be to sow discontent and frustration among segments of the workforce, which could only have negative consequences for the operation of the undertaking.

In any event, where collective agreements are binding, it is frequently laid down by law or held by the courts that the agreement supersedes individual contracts; at times the jurisprudence is that the relevant parts of the collective agreement are considered to be implicitly contained in the individual contract. In fact the latter approach has sometimes been used by courts to enforce the provisions of collective agreements in countries or situations where such agreements were not in themselves considered to be legally binding.

Still on this subject of variances from the collective agreement by way of individual arrangements, it is of interest to note that while more favourable individual arrangements are not frowned upon by the Recommendation, an attempt to provide such more favourable arrangements could give rise to difficulties under certain systems. This would of course not be the case where collective agreements merely lay down minimum standards, as is common where agreements cover a whole industry. However, in other countries, particularly where enterprise-level negotiations are common, collective bargaining and agreements treat of *actual* standards and managers might be ill-advised to offer better conditions unilaterally. In some cases, should this be done, it would be considered as an action subverting the position of the trade union in the enterprise, even leading to charges of sanctionable, illegal practices. Thus managers should exercise a degree of care when contemplating departures from the stipulations of collective agreements.

In addition to binding the parties, Recommendation No. 91 suggests that collective agreements should be binding for a given period of time. Indeed, it provides that national laws and regulations may call for a "minimum period during which, in the absence of any provision to the contrary in the agreement, collective agreements shall be deemed to be binding unless revised or rescinded at an earlier date by the parties". An agreed or imposed period of validity of a collective agreement is something that managers should welcome since it enhances the element of stability and predictability, and hence the possibilities to plan ahead as discussed earlier.

Recommendation No. 91 also endorses what should in any event be good managerial practice by providing that management should take appropriate steps to bring to the notice of the workers the text of applicable collective agreements. While some might contend that this should be a function of the trade union vis-à-vis its members (and it is certain that unions generally will take initiatives in this regard), it is nevertheless a managerial function to inform employees as to their terms and conditions of service. This becomes particularly important in managements' programmes of induction of new employees, and should constitute a basic precept of personnel management.

Enforcement of agreements

Recommendation No. 91 is not the only ILO instrument to address itself to the question of the nature and significance of collective agreements. The Collective Bargaining Recommendation, 1981 (No. 163), as well as Recommendation No. 91, both deal with disputes arising out of the application or interpretation of collective agreements. The latter instrument provides that such disputes "should be submitted to an appropriate procedure for settlement established either by agreement between the parties or by laws or regulations". This idea is echoed in Recommendation No. 163, which calls for measures adapted to national conditions to be taken so that procedures are available to this end. Moreover, the Examination of Grievances Recommendation, 1967 (No. 130), details a whole series of procedures and principles relating to adjustment of grievances, including grievances based on the claimed non-application of applicable collective agreements. Although the terms of Recommendation No. 130 will be considered further below, it may be noted here that the instrument envisages an "internal" procedure within the enterprise with the possibility of ultimate recourse for final adjustment to an outside authority, including arbitration bodies, labour courts, or judicial authorities.

The provisions of the three Recommendations in this regard of course are not entirely innovative. They at the same time seek to bolster the impact and usefulness of collective agreements and reflect desirable practice as witnessed by the experience of a great number of countries. In fact, it would make a mockery of the entire process of collective bargaining and the institution of collective agreements, as well as of the solemn pronouncements of the binding nature of agreements, if procedures were not available to ensure the proper application of the agreement, avoid violations of the agreement, and facilitate authoritative interpretations of the provisions of agreements where necessary. Thus, in line with the dispositions of the Recommendations referred to above, practice in many countries provides for final and binding decisions to be taken on questions of whether the parties are fulfilling their obligations under collective agreements. Where the agreements are binding in law as contracts, and in the absence of specialised procedures, recourse may be had by the aggrieved party to the normal courts. This brings into play all the trappings of legal procedures and judicial determination. In other countries a special judicial, or quasi-judicial, instance has been set up to handle disputes over the application or interpretation of collective agreements. Such labour courts or tribunals may sometimes have a wider jurisdiction, for example covering all labour disputes, whether they be over economic interests (such as deadlocks in collective bargaining as referred to above) or concern rights such as those deriving from an existing collective agreement or other established standard. However, in a number of countries the competence of such judicial or quasi-judicial bodies is limited to rights, and even more specifically, at times, to cases involving precisely the application or interpretation of collective agreements.

Adjustment of collective agreement disputes

A second approach to settlement of disputes of this type is that they be handled by arbitrators or arbitration bodies. We have already spoken of the use of arbitration with regard to final settlement of disputes arising out of deadlocks in collective bargaining. In certain countries the practice of arbitration is principally oriented towards the settlement of disputes over rights arising out of the interpretation and application of existing collective agreements. It is frequently a procedure that the parties themselves have agreed upon and included as a provision of the collective agreement. Moreover, it is often considered as the final stage in a grievance procedure involving successive steps within the enterprise or industry, resort to arbitration being had when the question is not settled within the internal grievance procedures. In fact, while some grievance and arbitration procedures are wider, in the practice of certain countries the concept of a "grievance" (and utilisation of the relevant procedures) is strictly limited to complaints of non-observance of the obligations of the collective agreement. And although the Examination of Grievances Recommendation refers to grievances in terms only of *workers'* complaints, resort to arbitration under grievance and arbitration procedures is often open, under provisions in collective agreements, to management as well. However, managerial recourse to arbitration, where possible, is rather rare (although far from unknown) since an alleged breach of the collective agreement by a worker usually leads to disciplinary action by management which, in turn, may be challenged by the worker or union concerned through the agreed grievance and arbitration procedure.

Where it is accepted that collective agreements are legally binding on the parties (and under some systems, to non-signatory parties under the doctrine of extension), why, it may be asked, has not the enforcement of the agreement been left to the regular courts? As stated, this is in fact sometimes the case. But in many industrial relations systems the industrial relations parties, or public policy, have determined that specialised procedures and institutions such as labour courts or arbitration are desirable. There have been three principal, and related, reasons for this view.

First is the question of expertise. When dealing with labour disputes arising out of the interpretation and application of collective agreements, decisions on the relative rights and obligations of the parties concerned must be illuminated by a certain knowledge of industrial relations and the work situation. There must also be an appreciation of the fact that, unlike commercial contracts, collective agreements are a reflection of a continuing relationship; and in industrial relations, unlike marriage, there is no divorce. It is clear that judges of labour courts or arbitrators will more surely have this perspective, or will gain it with experience, than will ordinary judges.

Secondly, the ordinary courts involve complicated rules of procedures and a degree of formalism which the alternative institutions discussed here normally eschew. Prime tenets of labour courts and arbitration are ease of access, a degree of informality and non-reliance on procedural or evidentiary rules. Among other things, this frequently avoids the need to bring in lawyers to represent the parties. Indeed, in some of these systems, lawyers as such are not permitted to appear.

Thirdly, and related to both of the first two points, is the idea of speed. The regular courts are often slow in dispensing justice, partly resulting from overcrowded calendars, and partly from the capacity for dilatory tactics under court procedures. Another prime tenet of the alternate institutions is the speedy disposition of cases. The dispatch with which they can handle cases is facilitated precisely by the degree of expertise and familiarity with industrial relations of the judges or arbitrators and the flexibility of procedures. And, in an industrial relations situation, speed is of the essence. If questions concerning the implementation of a collective agreement cannot be quickly and fairly resolved, relationships can deteriorate and the climate of the enterprise is adversely affected to the detriment of management, the workers and the community at large.

* * *

There is an additional point to be stressed in this discussion of collective agreements. It is widely, although not universally, considered that the conclusion of a collective agreement should obviate recourse to strikes or lock-outs for the period of the agreement. In principle, all matters have been negotiated and settled and any new matters should await new negotiations on the occasion of the termination of the existing agreement. And as seen immediately above, any controversy arising out of the application or interpretation of an existing agreement need not be settled by direct industrial action, but is rather subjected to the judicial or quasi-judicial procedures just discussed. ILO instruments in no way require a scenario such as that just described. But they do permit it and to a certain extent encourage it. Obviously enforcement of a *voluntary* relinquishment of the right to strike by unions would present no problem. But, additionally, the ILO supervisory bodies countenance legislative or judicial findings under which strikes would be illegal during the pendancy of a collective agreement even where the agreement itself does not speak to the point. In a sense the agreement is considered a counterpart for giving up a right to strike (or lock out) where there is adequate means for resolving questions of interpretation or application of the agreement. And from the point of view of the manager, a coherent system of industrial relations – even while guaranteeing basic rights and satisfactory conditions for workers – should include the reasonable expectation that he can operate his business without having to be concerned about possible work stoppages once agreement is reached with the union or once economic issues have been determined under a voluntary arbitration system.

Chapter 6

Consultation and communications

Although we have stressed the possibilities of collective bargaining providing the mechanism for mutual problem solving, there is no question that managers and trade unions meet to bargain in a largely adversarial, if not conflictual, setting. As opposed to the bargaining relationship, the emphasis in this chapter is on consultation, co-operation and communication, involving the treatment of questions of common interest to management, workers and the latter's representatives (both trade union representatives and other types of workers' representatives).

Consultation

A basic and underlying idea is that spelled out in the Co-operation at the Level of the Undertaking Recommendation, 1952 (No. 94). The Recommendation calls for the promotion of consultation in the enterprise on matters of mutual concern not dealt with in collective bargaining or other machinery concerned with the determination of terms and conditions of employment. The Recommendation further suggests the encouragement of such consultation through voluntary agreements between the parties. It also provides that consultation and co-operation may be promoted, as an alternative to or in combination with voluntary agreement, by laws or regulations establishing appropriate bodies for this purpose as well as their scope, functions and structure. The Recommendation, which is very brief, merely lays down the general principle without specifying details as to particular subjects for, or specific forms of, consultation and co-operation.

It is worth noting, even emphasising, that managers, where they take the initiative in introducing joint consultation schemes, should give some thought to the situation of the trade union with which it deals. History is replete with examples where reasonably sound industrial relations, or the possibility thereof, were compromised through management efforts to set up such machinery in circumstances where the union saw the efforts, rightly or wrongly, as a threat to their role and standing in the enterprise. And the Recommendation reflects this both by suggesting that the establishment of joint consultation result from agreement and that it not intrude into the domain par excellence of the trade union – collective bargaining.

At the present time it is more than ever necessary for managers to have systematised and constant access to the views of the workers and their representatives on questions of common interest. Rapidly changing technology, efforts to improve the quality of working life (including the introduction of new or changed forms of work organisation), the life and death struggle to maintain and increase productivity, and many other current issues lend themselves to, indeed cry out for, joint consultation if the equilibrium and harmony of the workplace is to be maintained and the individual and collective genius of the workforce is to be tapped.

Communications

To achieve these ends – and working from the principle of joint consultation – managers will have to sharpen their techniques of communications within the enterprise. Numerous specialised handbooks and courses are available on the subject of communications but it is useful to know that the International Labour Conference, in the Communications within the Undertaking Recommendation, 1967 (No. 129), actually set out elements for an enterprise communications policy. The Recommendation calls attention to the importance, in the common interest of both management and labour, of a climate of mutual understanding and trust which can be promoted by the rapid provision – and exchange – of information relating to the life of the enterprise. Thus, under the terms of the Recommendation, management, *after consultation with workers' representatives*, should adopt an effective communications policy. This policy should ensure that the provision of relevant information, and consultation itself, takes place before management takes decisions on matters of major interest, in so far as disclosure of the information in question will not prejudice either party.

The first element of a communications policy to be mentioned is that it should be adapted to the nature of the enterprise, also taking account of the size, composition and interests of the workforce. Additional elements are that there should be two-way communications between management and the workers on the one hand and, on the other, between the head of the enterprise, the personnel manager or other representative of top management and the trade union representative (or others having the responsibility of workers' representation pursuant to national law or practice or collective agreement).

The policy should reflect the idea that where management wishes to transmit information through union (or other workers') representatives, the representatives should be given the means to do so. Moreover, management should see that their communications policy does not, through the communications channels used, weaken the poition of either supervisors or workers' representatives. In other words, there is certain information that should come from or through the supervisors and not over their head or behind their back, for this would compromise their status and standing in the eyes of those working under the supervisors' direction. Similarly, it would be a mistake in given cases to communicate directly with union members, or the workers more generally, rather than using the conduit of the union representative or other workers' representatives. Few things can be more detrimental to union-management, and hence to sound labour-management, relations in the enterprise than seeking to communicate directly with the workforce on matters which are of direct and immediate concern to the trade union, particularly where these matters, under prevailing practice, should first be discussed with the union.

Other elements of the communications policy include a non-exhaustive list of the communications media that may be utilised: informational meetings; documentary materials aimed at specific groups (such as supervisors' bulletins and personnel policy manuals); mass communications media such as house journals, newsletters, notice boards, exhibitions, visits, films, film strips and slides, radio and television; and media geared to garnering suggestions and ideas of the workers.

As to the substance of communications, one element of the policy is that it should include all matters of interest to the workers relating to the operation and future prospects of the enterprise and to the present and future situation of the workers "in so far as disclosure of the information will not cause damage to the parties". The Recommendation then goes on to cite specific elements of information which management should give, as follows:

(a) general conditions of employment, including engagement, transfer and termination of employment;

(b) job descriptions and the place of particular jobs within the structure of the undertaking;

(c) possibilities of training and prospects of advancement within the undertaking;

(d) general working conditions;

(e) occupational safety and health regulations and instructions for the prevention of accidents and occupational diseases;

(f) procedures for the examination of grievances as well as the rules and practices governing their operation and the conditions for having recourse to them;

(g) personnel welfare services (medical care, health, canteens, housing, leisure, savings and banking facilities, etc.);

(h) social security or social assistance schemes in the undertaking;

(i) the regulations of national social security schemes in the undertaking;

(j) the general situation of the undertaking and prospects or plans for its future development;

(k) the explanation of decisions which are likely to affect directly or indirectly the situation of workers in the undertaking;

(l) methods of consultation and discussion and of co-operation between management and its representatives on the one hand and the workers and their representatives on the other.

The Recommendation cautions that information which has been the subject of negotiations or of a collective agreement should be identified as such.

In sum, ILO standards recognise that communication, and communications policies, are an essential management interest. This is of course reflected in practice by the fact that great emphasis is given to this area by management and that communications are considered widely to be a key function of personnel management. The ideas, information, indeed warnings, contained in Recommendation No. 129 can very well serve, and are intended to serve, as a direct inspiration for managers wishing to develop or improve their enterprises' communications policies and activities.

Chapter 7

The manager and general conditions of employment

A later chapter is devoted to the manager and the personnel function, but in this chapter attention will be focused on those international standards which deal with some particular aspects of general conditions of work, including hours of work, weekly rest periods, wages, holidays with pay, and paid educational leave. In carrying out his job, a manager will be regularly confronted with questions and problems concerning these subjects. International standards do not always give precise guide-lines about what to do or what not to do but they certainly have an influence on the policies of national governments and of trade unions. It is, therefore, important for a manager to have an idea of the international standards in these fields since they can have an impact on his day-to-day work.

Hours of work

The very first international labour standard dealt with hours of work. This is not surprising, because in the first part of the twentieth century there was a strong movement in most industrialised countries in favour of a compulsory reduction in working hours. The eight-hour day had for many years been among the most important objectives of trade unions and a number of political parties. In October 1919, at its First Session, the International Labour Conference adopted a Convention (No. 1) limiting the hours of work in industrial undertakings to eight in the day and to 48 in the week. The term "industrial undertakings" was used in a broad sense, but did not include commercial establishments.

There were whole classes of workers which, for one reason or another, had to be exempted from the limit of 48 hours because of the special nature of their employment or the special conditions of the industry. These included workers whose duties required their presence before and after ordinary working hours or whose duties were of an exceptionally light kind, or who worked in industries of a seasonable nature, or whose materials were perishable. The Convention provides that the public authority has to determine these permanent and temporary exceptions and the regulations to deal with them (but only after consultation with organisations of workers and employers, if these existed), including fixing the maximum amount of overtime, while the minimum overtime pay rate was to be time and a quarter.

Convention No. 1 came into force in June 1921, but ratification was not forthcoming in many countries. Firstly this was because adoption came at a time that a number of European countries had turned all their energy to the task of recovering from the devastation of the war. Secondly, in many countries ratification required a radical change in attitude of those in power, who had long based their action on the principles of economic liberalism and non-intervention by the State. Certain countries were also afraid that their ratification of the Convention would have unfavourable effects for their industries resulting from competition by countries that did not ratify the Convention.

There have been some significant interpretations of the Convention and particularly as regards temporary exceptions to its provisions. The Committee of Experts has pointed out that "temporary exceptions to normal hours of work are allowed only so that establishments may deal with exceptional cases of pressure of work and that the maximum of additional hours authorised must be fixed after consultation with the organisations of employers and workers". It furthermore observed that the legislative provision, "under which normal hours of work may be extended if the work is required for development purposes or with a view to increasing production, is not in conformity with the Convention, which authorises temporary exceptions only to enable establishments to deal with exceptional cases of pressure of work".

The Hours of Work (Commerce and Offices) Convention, 1930 (No. 30), limits the hours of work to 48 in the week and eight in the day and applies to persons employed in commercial and trading establishments; establishments and administrative services in which the persons employed are mainly engaged in office work, and mixed commercial and industrial establishments unless these are considered as industrial undertakings. It does not apply to persons working in medical institutions, hotels, theatres, etc.

The subsequent international labour standards in the field of working hours reflect the developments in a number of countries with regard to hours of work or the concern for employment. The International Labour Conference discussed the reduction of weekly working hours in 1935. One of the main reasons was that "unemployment has become so widespread and long continued that there are at the present time many millions of workers throughout the world suffering hardship and privation for which they are not themselves responsible and from which they are justly entitled to be relieved".

A second consideration was that workers should as far as practicable be enabled to share in the benefits of the rapid technical progress in modern industry. On the basis of these and other considerations, the Conference adopted the Forty-Hour Week Convention, 1935 (No. 47). This is a very brief instrument which, in a sense, does not announce mandatory general standards as such, but merely calls on States ratifying the Convention to declare their "approval" of the principle of a 40-hour week and to take measures appropriate to secure this end. Application of the principle of a 40-hour week is to be in such a manner that standards of living are not reduced in consequence. It is interesting to note that member States were so slow to ratify this Convention, adopted in 1935, that it did not come into force until 1951.

In the early 1960s working hours were once again placed on the agenda of the International Labour Conference. After lengthy discussions (three years were needed), the Reduction of Hours of Work Recommendation (No. 116) was adopted in 1962. The Recommendation was designed to supplement and facilitate the implementation of the already existing international instruments concerning working hours. The 40-hour week was recommended as a social standard to be reached by stages if necessary. Another principle of the Recommendation is that normal hours of work should progressively be reduced without any reductions in the wages of the workers.

The Recommendation met with great opposition from the employers, not so much because they were opposed to a reduction of hours of work whenever possible, but because of their great concern at the prospect of an instrument fixing normal hours of work at 40 a week, which Convention No. 47, as noted above, specifically did not do. They were of the opinion that the scope for reducing working hours varied so much from country to country, and even within the same country from industry to industry, that a further attempt to reduce hours of work at the international level was not likely to prove fruitful. It might, in fact, hamper efforts to increase productivity in countries that were just beginning to industrialise. The employers, however, were ultimately willing to endorse the idea of a 40-hour week as an objective to be worked towards in the future.

Weekly rest periods

Weekly rest periods are directly related to hours of work. ILO action in this respect started in 1921 when the Conference adopted a Convention concerning the application of the weekly rest in industrial undertakings (No. 14). As a rule workers are to enjoy an uninterrupted rest period of at least 24 consecutive hours in every seven-day period. To the extent possible, the period of rest is to coincide with days of rest traditional to the country.

Questions related to the interpretation and application of these provisions can pose problems for managers. For example, the Committee of Experts, with regard to legislative provisions that persons working on a compulsory rest day could choose between compensatory rest and payment in cash, noted that this choice could be authorised only where the worker is called on to work *exceptionally* on the weekly day of rest and that such solution, as an exception, was not contrary to the provision of the Convention, which authorises in certain cases exceptions to the principle of weekly rest.

Also in 1921, the Conference adopted the Weekly Rest (Commerce) Recommendation (No. 18), which in 1957 was superseded by Convention No. 106, supplemented by Recommendation No. 103, concerning weekly rest in commerce and offices. Convention No. 106 also provides for an uninterrupted weekly rest period of not less than 24 hours in the course of each period of seven days and that, where possible, the weekly rest period is to coincide with the day of the week established as a day of rest by national or local traditions or customs.

The Recommendation, however, reflects changes in practice and recommends an uninterrupted weekly rest period of not less than 36 hours which, wherever practicable, should be calculated to include the period from midnight to midnight and not to include other rest periods immediately preceding or following the weekly rest period.

The application of Convention No. 106 regularly gives rise to questions regarding the categories of workers covered by this Convention. In 1981 for instance, the Committee of Experts observed that the Convention applies to temporary workers employed for a period of not more than six months and to workers in enterprises employing fewer than five workers. Another observation has to do with a provision which ensures that persons who work on the weekly day of rest are to receive a compensatory rest period of 24 consecutive hours during the following seven days, irrespective of any compensatory wage.

It may be recalled that, while these standards on rest periods imply obligations for ratifying countries, they also reflect minimum standards of good practice for employers and managers.

Minimum wages

A key aspect of the employment relationship is the wage paid for work performed. For various reasons the question of wages is of importance to workers, employers, managers and governments. In a large number of countries actual wage rates are negotiated between employers or their organisations and trade unions (or other workers' representatives), although the level of bargaining may vary from country to country – plant, enterprise, industry, or even national level – as discussed in the chapter on collective bargaining.

The fixing of wage rates, however, becomes more of a problem in those branches of economic activity in which no arrangements exist for the effective regulation of wages by collective agreements. One of the reasons for the lack of such arrangements can be the absence of representative trade unions, for instance in the home working trades, or because of an exceptionally low degree of unionisation in the particular industry or trade.

To protect those workers as well as workers in sectors with particularly low wages, the government may feel the need to assume responsibility and create machinery for the fixing of minimum wages in the sectors concerned.

The International Labour Organisation has displayed considerable circumspection in dealing with the question of wages because of the economic repercussions that this may entail. Nevertheless, several international instruments have been adopted over the years with regard to various aspects of wages. Such instruments may not always be of immediate concern to managers, but in many countries managers will certainly have to deal with the outcome of minimum wage fixing which may have direct or indirect impact on wages in their own sectors. Conventions in this field generally represent a form of action to promote and guide the work of appropriate tripartite or joint wage-fixing institutions, i.e. that of employers' and workers' organisations with or without participation of the public authorities, with a view to ensuring the application of a particular national wage policy.

The International Labour Conference has so far adopted the following instruments: the Minimum Wage-Fixing Machinery Convention, 1928 (No. 26); the Minimum Wage-Fixing Machinery (Agriculture) Convention, 1951 (No. 99); and Convention No. 131 and Recommendation No. 135 concerning minimum wage fixing with special reference to developing countries, 1970. These Conventions provide for the creation or maintenance of machinery whereby minimum rates of wages can be fixed for workers employed in trades and occupations in which no arrangements exist for the effective regulation of wages by collective agreement or otherwise and wages are exceptionally low. All of the instruments provide for consultation of representative employers' and workers' organisations prior to setting up wage-fixing machinery. Convention No. 131 emphasises the need for governments to consult fully with representative employers' and workers' organisations: firstly to determine the groups of wage earners to be covered; and secondly to associate employers' and workers' organisations or, where no such organisations exist, representatives of employers and workers concerned, in the operation of the machinery in equal numbers and on equal terms.

While Conventions Nos. 26 and 99 do not give criteria for the level of minimum wages, Convention No. 131 indicates elements that should be taken into consideration such as the needs of the workers and their families, the general level of wages in the country, the cost of living, social security benefits and the relative living standard of other social groups as well as economic factors, including the requirements of economic development, levels of productivity and the desirability of attaining and maintaining a high level of employment.

Convention No. 99 provides for the possibility, in the agricultural sector, of authorising partial payment of minimum wages in the form of allowances in kind in cases in which such payment is customary or desirable. Such allowances should be appropriate for the personal use and benefit of the worker and his family and their value should be fair and reasonable.

Governments ratifying these Conventions assume the obligation to inform the employers and workers concerned of the minimum wage rates in force and to ensure the actual payment of these rates.

Recommendation No. 135 calls for the adoption of criteria which will make systems of minimum wages in developing countries both an effective instrument of social protection and an element in the strategy of economic and social development. It also stresses that minimum wage fixing should not operate to the prejudice of the exercise and growth of free collective bargaining as a means of fixing wages higher than the minimum.

Law and practice on minimum wage fixing have frequently given rise to observations by the Committee of Experts. With regard to Convention No. 26, for instance, the Committee pointed out that the Convention provides that the competent authorities may authorise payment of wages below the fixed minimum when such lower wages are laid down by collective agreement. However, the decree under examination by the Committee specified that in the event of economic instability of an enterprise, the minimum wage fixing body could authorise employers to pay wages below the legal minimum, without restricting this possibility to cases approved by collective agreements. The decree was found to raise problems of conformity with the Convention and was consequently amended.

Protection of wages

The Convention concerning the protection of wages, 1949 (No. 95), supplemented by the Recommendation (No. 85) of the same year on that subject, is of interest to managers since it deals with items relating to remuneration methods and other concerns that are frequently functions of personnel departments.

The Convention starts out by defining the term "wages" as meaning remuneration or earnings, however designed or calculated, capable of being expressed in terms of money and fixed by agreement, law or regulations, resulting from a contract of employment for work or services done or rendered.

Many of the provisions of the Convention are of direct importance to managers because they are meant to protect the workers against arbitrary action by management which may influence the worker's freedom to dispose of his wages. The Convention for instance allows under certain conditions partial payment of wages in kind, but not in the form of liquor of high alcoholic content, a practice customary in certain countries for workers in the spirits industry. The interpretation of what should be considered as payment in legal tender can present difficulties (the Convention provides that wages payable in money shall be paid only in "legal tender"): in 1981 the Committee of Experts found legislation in conflict with the Convention which provided that harvest workers on coffee plantations could receive substitutes for cash, which substitutes, according to the government concerned, were convertible into legal tender and were not means of payment but of control of production.

The right of workers to dispose freely of their wages as provided by the Convention can be limited by the practice of giving advances on wages at the time of recruitment. This practice is related to the problem of the terms of repayment of debts incurred, particularly by agricultural workers. The Convention provides that the conditions and extent of deductions must be prescribed by national laws or fixed by agreements.

Recommendation No. 85 suggests limitations with regard to deductions from wages. For instance, the reimbursement of loss or damage to equipment are to be authorised only where the worker concerned is clearly responsible and the amounts withheld fair. Deductions from wages in respect of tools and equipment supplied by the employer should be limited to cases where such deductions are a recognised custom or provided for by collective agreement, arbitration award or otherwise authorised (through national laws or regulations).

Periodicity of wage payments is fixed at not less than twice a month for hourly, daily or weekly paid workers and no less than once a month for those paid on a monthly or annual basis. Notification to the workers of wage conditions is provided for, particularly as regards rates, periodicity and method of calculation. Workers are to be informed with each payment of wages of the gross amount, deductions and their nature, and the net amount.

It would seem clear that the conditions set out in the instruments on protection of wages reflect a reasonable approach to certain aspects of wage and salary administration (more of which will be discussed later) which in turn is a cardinal aspect of personnel management.

Holidays with pay

Over the years the International Labour Conference has adopted a series of international labour standards dealing with holidays with pay: Convention No. 52 and Recommendation No. 47 concerning annual holidays with pay, 1936; Convention No. 101 and Recommendation No. 93 concerning holidays with pay in agriculture, 1952; Recommendation No. 98 concerning holidays with pay, 1954; and Convention No. 132 concerning annual holidays with pay (revised), 1970.

In line with general ILO philosophy, the development of improved conditions in this respect should be sought through the encouragement by governments of voluntary action or agreements between employers' and workers' organisations. However, if this action does not give speedy and satisfactory results, governments are called upon to adopt appropriate laws or regulations.

The main provisions of the Conventions concerning annual holidays with pay reflect the rapid development in many countries with regard to the length of annual holidays. In 1936 Convention No. 52 provided for at least six working days per year, in 1954 Recommendation No. 98 called for two weeks, whereas in 1970 Convention No. 132 provided for no less than three working weeks' annual holidays with pay (subject to an allowable minimum period of service of not more than six months).

The annual holiday may be divided into parts but one of the parts should consist of at least two uninterrupted weeks. Exceptions to this rule may, however, be provided through collective agreements. The employer may determine the time at which the holiday shall be taken – unless it is fixed by regulation or agreement – in consultation with the employees concerned or with their representatives. In fixing the holiday time, the work requirements and the opportunities for rest and relaxation available to the employee are to be taken into account.

Certain provisions of the relevant instruments have given rise to differences in interpretation. In a case where legislation allowed the postponement of annual holiday to the following year in exceptional circumstances and gave the right to accumulate holidays for a maximum of three years under certain circumstances, the Committee of Experts pointed out that under Convention No. 52 the minimum period of six working days has to be taken every year. Any other interpretation, the Committee held, would conflict with the intention of the Conference which, when it adopted the Convention, removed from the draft a specific provision laying down, as an exceptional measure, the postponement of the annual holiday to a later year.

Paid educational leave

Somewhat related to annual leave with pay is the subject of paid educational leave. This subject could also be discussed in relation with human resources development (see Chapter 9) but here the emphasis is on the leave element.

In 1974 the Conference adopted Convention No. 140 and Recommendation No. 148 concerning paid educational leave. Some of the ideas underlying the adoption of these instruments included the affirmation in the Universal Declaration of Human Rights that everyone has a right to education and that, in a rapidly changing society, there was a need for continuing education. The Convention calls on governments to formulate and apply a policy to promote the granting of paid educational leave for the purpose of training at any level and of general, social, civic and trade union education. Employers' and workers' organisations as well as educational and training institutions should be associated with the formulation of such a policy.

The Recommendation emphasises that workers should be encouraged to take the greatest advantage of available education and training facilities and employers should be encouraged to grant educational leave to their workers.

Contributions to the financing of paid educational leave may be expected from public authorities, employers and their organisations, workers' organisations and educational institutions.

It is recommended that priority be given to certain categories of workers, or particular functions or occupations, whose educational or training needs are especially urgent given, among other things, the requirements of the undertaking. As regards trade union education, the Recommendation provides that the trade unions concerned should be responsible for selecting candidates.

The financial entitlements of workers, participating in an educational leave programme, should maintain their level of earnings and also take into account any major additional costs of education or training.

The Committee of Experts has taken note that, apart from training of trade union representatives where provided by statute, recent surveys tended to show that in a number of countries paid educational leave is much more likely to be provided for professional employees, where it is seen to be an integral part of their work; for public servants, bank, finance and other white-collar commercial employees, where it is more or less an accepted condition of work;

or for apprentices in the skilled occupations and for technicians, where formally structured off-the-job training is seen as a more effective form of training. The Committee considered that the scope and possibilities of paid educational leave could be broadened beyond those mentioned.

Chapter 8

The manager and physical conditions of work

The aspect of physical conditions of work that is perhaps of greatest concern to managers at all levels is that of occupational safety and health and the creation of a working environment in which optimal working conditions can be assured.

Notwithstanding the considerable progress that has been made in this field, it has been estimated that over 100,000 people are killed every year and a further 1.5 million are incapacitated by work-related accidents. With the progress of industrialisation and recent technological advances, new hazards are created affecting both the safety and the health of workers everywhere. The increasing complexity of work brought about by these innovations and the rising incidence of work-related problems has resulted in a renewed interest in questions of safety and health and the working environment, an interest which found expression in the 1970s in industrialised countries in the formulation of new laws (or the extensive revision of existing laws) and national policies directed towards the creation of a safer and healthier working environment.

It is hardly necessary to point out that safety and health and, more generally, the working environment, should be of vital concern to managers from at least two practical and related points of view, both concerning directly or indirectly labour costs and their reduction. And here we would leave aside, for the moment, basic humanitarian considerations which in any event would motivate managers to be concerned with safety and health and the working environment.

First, although measures taken by management in these areas often (but not always) have a price tag, managers should recognise the fact that not taking adequate steps to protect and promote the safety and health of employees can have an even greater price tag. According to estimates made in the late 1970s for industrialised countries alone, the average overall cost of work-related accidents and illness amounted to some four per cent of gross national product. The cost in developing countries could well be greater. It is clear that a good percentage of these costs, in terms of benefits paid, loss of production and of productivity, damage to material and equipment, etc., must be borne by the employer.

Secondly, in dealing with more general questions of the working environment and its improvement – that is, adapting work to the worker and sometimes referred to as humanisation of work – there can also be a handsome pay-off for the enterprise. In fact, managers sometimes speak of the "double pay-off" in this regard, reflecting greater job satisfaction for the worker and consequent better productivity for the enterprise.

The ILO's own preoccupation with physical conditions of work and occupational safety and health goes back to the early days of the organisation and has been reflected in a number of different ways. Apart from its quite considerable standard-setting activities (which will be dealt with below), the Organisation has undertaken a number of other activities designed to promote the improvement of working conditions and occupational safety and health. Its efforts in this direction include tripartite meetings of industrial and analogous committees and groups of experts, research and publications, the collection, analysis and dissemination of information, seminars and courses for employers and workers and technical co-operation projects and programmes. It has also formulated and published a long series of codes of practice and guides on specific aspects of occupational safety and health and its *Encyclopaedia on Occupational Safety and Health* and Occupational Safety and Health Series constitute invaluable sources of reference in this field. Since 1959 its International Occupational Safety and Health Information Centre (CIS) has been active in the dissemination of information and in 1976 the ILO Governing Body approved the setting up of an International Programme for the Improvement of Working Conditions and Environment (PIACT). The idea underlying the latter is that the traditionally separate fields of occupational safety and health and conditions of work should be closely linked and seen from a wider perspective that included not only the protection of workers but also the improvement of the working environment and of the quality of working life.

This trend towards a wider concept of the physical conditions of work is as readily apparent in the Organisation's standard-setting activities and in particular in its Convention and Recommendation concerning occupational safety and health and the working environment adopted in 1981 (referred to below as Convention No. 155 and Recommendation No. 164). Convention No. 155 indeed speaks of national policies which should take account of "relationships between the material elements of work and the persons who carry out or supervise the work, and adaptation of machinery, equipment, working time, organisation of work and work processes to the physical and mental capacities of the workers".

But the ILO's standard-setting activities with regard to occupational safety and health go as far back as the earliest sessions of the International Labour Conference when it adopted Recommendations No. 3, concerning the prevention of anthrax, and No. 4, concerning the protection of women and children against lead poisoning (at its First Session, in 1919), and Convention No. 13, concerning the use of white lead in painting (at its Third Session, in 1921). However, except for the Recommendations concerning the prevention of industrial accidents, 1929 (No. 31), the protection of the health of workers in places of employment, 1953 (No. 97), and occupational health services in places of employment, 1959 (No. 112), the instruments adopted by the ILO on the subject of safety and health have tended to deal either with specific sectors of economic activity (e.g. docks, building, etc.) or with specific subjects (e.g.

occupational cancer, the guarding of machinery, labour inspection, etc.). The trend towards a more comprehensive treatment of the subject has only become apparent since the 1970s, a development reflected in some of the recent resolutions adopted by the Conference, in the setting up of PIACT in 1976 and in the formulation and adoption of Convention No. 155 and Recommendation No. 164 (see below).

While it is evident that many of the ILO's instruments in the area of occupational safety and health will be of interest to particular groups of managers, given their relatively specific nature and the wider audience of this guide, this chapter will concentrate on those Conventions and Recommendations of a more general nature and a wider applicability. Particular attention will be paid to Convention No. 155 and Recommendation No. 164 as they might correctly be described as representing an attempt to pull together the ILO's previous work in the area and to provide a broad, general and, above all, flexible framework within which national governments and the social partners can work towards an optimal level of safety and health in all workplaces.

As the above indicates, Convention No. 155 and Recommendation No. 164, concerning occupational safety and health and the working environment, differ from previous ILO instruments regarding the subject by virtue of their more global nature. Their importance lies specifically in the fact that they establish basic objectives and define the principles of a coherent policy on occupational hazards, on improving the working environment and, as mentioned earlier, adapting work to the human being. This represents a radical departure from the traditional concept of occupational safety and health and necessitates a number of changes in the conceptualisation of the roles of the various actors involved and in workplace relations, both of which must undoubtedly have a considerable impact on the day-to-day work of managers at all levels.

In recent years there has been a new development in occupational health and safety policy, namely the desire, as alluded to above, to make work more human; to adapt work to the workers and not vice versa. In many countries it is no longer considered sufficient to protect workers from a hostile and dehumanising environment or to protect them from accidents and health hazards. Rather, there is a growing tendency to improve the work environment to make it less hostile and more human – and to relate its technological and social elements more closely to those of the society in which it exists.

Within this wider conceptualisation of working conditions, occupational health means more than the absence of disease or infirmity. As Convention No. 155 indicates, it also includes the physical and mental elements which affect health. In the context of this standard – and of some of the most recent national legislation – occupational health is, therefore, defined as a condition of complete physical, mental and social well-being, a concept which the ILO tried to promote 30 years ago. Similarly, it is recognised that safety questions are not a single, easily isolated problem, but that they demand the consideration of a whole complex of issues ranging from the design of buildings and equipment to manpower characteristics, work relations and the quality of working life.

Seen from the standpoint of safety and health, the "working environment", stressed in Convention No. 155 and Recommendation No. 164, thus becomes a question of the interplay of individuals, equipment, substances or agents and operating procedures. Choices of technology and processes, decisions on location and layout of plants, choices of systems and working procedures, the organisation of work and industrial relations, all become determinants of the idea that working environment and safety and health at the workplace are greatly influenced by the decisions taken at the successive stages in production, design and organisation. The extent to which jobs can be adapted to workers' physical, mental and social needs depends on how these options are exercised by management and on how decisions are made. To be effective, an occupational safety and health programme must be a global process based on feedback and learning and involving the mutual adaptation of the various components of the working environment. It must, therefore, go well beyond the traditional model of the discovery of shortcomings, their relation to existing rules and the application of corrective measures. While the two basic methods identified by the Protection of Workers' Health Recommendation, 1953 (No. 97), i.e. technical measures for hazard control and medical surveillance of individual workers, are still valid, managers must recognise that enduring safe working conditions for workers and a meaningful employment situation for every worker involves a much wider range of factors than was previously appreciated. The manager's own role in this process is rendered all the more important because the complexity of the modern work environment leads to a situation where "control" or supervision in this area has to be "inside the system itself". It can no longer be left exclusively to outside bodies, such as the labour inspectorate, with no possibility of constantly following complex events and changing relationships at the workplace. This is a fact which the recent legislation referred to above clearly recognised when it shifted its emphasis from the national level to that of the undertaking.

General policies

Convention No. 155 calls on member States of the ILO to "formulate, implement and periodically review a coherent national policy on occupational safety, occupational health and the working environment", the aim of which would be "to prevent accidents and injury to health arising out of, linked with or occurring in the course of work, by minimising, so far as is reasonably practicable, the causes of hazards inherent in the working environment". As measures taken pursuant to national policies embodying these precepts, by statute or otherwise, have a direct impact on and relevance to the work of managers at the level of the enterprise, it is worthwhile examining briefly the nature of regulations, the ways in which they affect the day-to-day activities of managers and the part, if any, that managers can play in their formulation.

By providing managers with a frame of reference within which to base their actions in the field of occupational safety and health and the working environment, by setting certain constraints and limitations on their actions through standards and codes of practice, and by providing for compliance with those standards, national law and regulations and other means of giving effect to the relevant national policies, have a considerable impact on the role and the day-to-day activities of managers. The Convention, for example, calls for consideration to be given to a number of spheres of action which generally fall within the competence and responsibility of managers. These include the design, testing, choice, substitution, installation, arrangements, use and maintenance of the material elements of work (e.g. workplaces, tools, work processes, etc.); the organisation of the relationships between these material arrangements and the persons who carry out or supervise the work; and, as mentioned earlier, the adaptation of machinery, equipment, working time and the organisation of work and work processes to the physical and mental capacities of workers. The Convention also calls for standards regarding the design, construction and layout of undertakings, their operations, the determination of work processes and of substances to which exposure should be limited. It might, therefore, be argued, and some employers do argue, that such requirements have a constraining effect and interfere with their management of the enterprise. A French Ministry of Labour circular (1965) on the prevention of occupational accidents and diseases presented an effective counter-argument. The circular states that:

> What must be said and, if necessary, be reiterated to employers who might complain of the burden of the regulations is that it is up to them to apply boldly, whether by steps taken within their undertaking or through active participation in outside safety organisations, those effective measures of prevention which ... will alone make it possible to relieve the pressure of statutory requirements and even to simplify their content.

It has also been argued with force that there are advantages in having clearly defined responsibilities for both managers and workers, competent guidance in complying with legal obligations (specifically provided for by Convention No. 155) and a set of instructions and standards for both managers and workers aimed at avoiding potential hazards or at neutralising hazards which cannot be eliminated. Limitations through regulatory means, and codes of practice, can serve to alert managers to potential hazards, thus helping them to avoid costly mistakes both in economic and in human terms. It has been estimated that the number of work-related accidents would amount to a small fraction of their present figures if enterprises consistently applied the recommended standards, in the interests of good practice if nothing else. An enterprise whose preventive measures show consistently good results is also an efficient and profitable firm and there appears to be a close relationship between a high level of safety and the quality of labour-management relations, communications and the psycho-social climate within an undertaking. A safe and healthy work environment can also have a positive effect on worker satisfaction and therefore on absenteeism, productivity and quality, all of which constitute sound economic motives for its creation and maintenance within the framework of the statutory provisions.

What role do managers have in the formulation of these policies and laws which affect them? Directly, a manager has little chance of influencing action at the national level. However, it is recognised that the formulation and implementation of a safety and health policy worthy of that name requires that there should be a community of views as to the priority aims and the measures to be applied. Thus Convention No. 155 provides for "consultation with the most representative organisations of employers and workers" in the formulation, implementation and periodic review of national policies. Recommendation No. 154 further states that there should be close co-operation between public authorities and representative employers' and workers' organisations, as well as other bodies concerned in the measures for the formulation and application of the policy referred to in the Convention. Thus, national policy, laws and regulations concerning occupational safety and health should, in principle, reflect the views of employers and managers who have the possibility of making their views known at the national level through their organisations. A number of recent national-level institutions for the promotion of occupational safety and health bear witness to the recognition and wide application of the principle of tripartism. These include the Health and Safety Commission in the United Kingdom, the Work Environment Commission in Sweden, the Canadian Centre for Occupational Health and Safety and the tripartite national committees or national safety councils or associations in a number of developing countries. Within these bodies managers directly, or through the relevant employers' associations, can indeed have their views taken into account in the formulation of occupational safety and health policies.

One provision of Convention No. 155 requires that the "enforcement of laws and regulations concerning occupational safety and health and the working environment shall be secured by an adequate and appropriate system of inspection". Elaborating on this provision, Recommendation No. 164 refers to the international labour Convention concerning labour inspection in industry and commerce, 1947 (No. 81), which specifies the characteristics and functions of such a service and is, therefore, of considerable interest to managers who are directly implicated in the process outlined.

Basically, the functions of the system of labour inspection as set out in Convention No. 81 are:

(a) to secure the enforcement of the legal provisions relating to conditions of work and the protection of workers while engaged in their work (including hours, safety and health and welfare);

(b) to supply technical information and advice to employers concerning the most effective means of complying with the legal provisions; and

(c) to bring to the notice of the competent authority defects and abuses not specifically covered by existing legal provisions.

In pursuit of these duties, labour inspectors are empowered inter alia, under the Convention, to enter freely and without previous notice, at any hour of the day or night, any workplace liable to inspection. The same provision also allows them considerable leeway in obtaining the requisite information regarding the observation of standards. Inspectors are also empowered to take steps to remedy defects in plant, layout or working methods which may constitute a threat to the health and safety of workers. Another provision stipulates that the labour inspectorate be notified of industrial accidents and cases of occupational disease. A provision which provides for legal proceedings against persons violating or neglecting to observe legal provisions leaves the choice between warning and advice and the institution of such proceedings to the inspector.

While at first glance the functions of the labour inspection system and the provisions for implementation undoubtedly impinge on the manager's functions and powers and might well be considered as allowing for undue intervention in the affairs of the undertaking by an outside authority, an efficient and effective system of labour inspection has much to recommend itself to managers, as well as to workers. In the first instance the system serves the very useful function of monitoring safety and health in undertakings and as such it serves as a useful back-up service to management's eventual economic advantage – of preventing accidents that are costly both in human and in material terms. As mentioned earlier, recent estimates in the industrialised countries demonstrate that the overall cost of industrial accidents is equivalent to around 4 per cent of GNP.

The system can also be useful in that it can offer both managers and workers invaluable technical advice concerning the most effective means of complying with existing legislation, the provision of which, again, can have a positive impact on the working environment. In addition, labour inspectorates also offer other important services to managers. The preventative duties of labour inspectors, as outlined in Recommendation No. 81, include the requirement of prior notice of the opening of an industrial or commercial establishment and the submission of plans regarding plants or processes of production enabling the service to advise employers on whether the plans would render difficult or impossible their compliance with national laws and regulations. While the inspector may have the right to order alterations, it must be recognised that revisions at the planning stage can be far less costly than alterations to established plants or the cost of industrial accidents and/or penalties. This is particularly so as penalties for non-compliance with statutory regulations are becoming more severe in a number of countries and can even include imprisonment for the manager concerned. In some countries too the reasons for imposition of penalties are increasing in scope and the criminal liability of the head of the undertaking tends to be more frequently raised in the case of fatal accidents due to negligence or wilful failure to take precautions, and not only due to breaches of safety regulations as was the case earlier. Furthermore, an inexcusable fault on the part of the employer is no longer the sole objective of investigation – even a simple failure of a line manager to take elementary precautions may now be seen as an infringement of regulations and is open to sanctions.

The duties of labour inspectors also include the encouragement of arrangements for collaboration of management and workers either directly, or through conferences, joint committees and other such bodies, and the imparting of advice and instruction to management and workers on labour legislation and questions of industrial safety and hygiene.

While in most developing countries the understaffed labour inspectorates may have difficulty in coping even with their primary function of inspection, in the developed countries it has been estimated that labour inspectors devote a growing proportion of their time to their advisory functions of persuading, educating and advising employers and workers and their organisations. As a result the application of regulations is tending to become a co-operative task – a feature which is very much in line with the principle of collaboration and co-operation underlying the provisions of Convention No. 155, and indeed much of the ILO's work.

Enterprise-level measures

It is evident that those provisions of Convention No. 155, and other international standards that relate to action at the level of the enterprise, will be of more direct relevance (and therefore of greater interest) to managers at all levels in so far as they have a greater influence and impact on their day-to-day work.

While international labour Conventions and Recommendations, by virtue of their international character and their objective of providing general guide-lines for national legislation and practice, devote somewhat more attention to action at the national level, the most recent and most advanced national legislation in the safety and health field demonstrates a marked shift towards creating a basis for enterprises themselves to deal directly with questions of safety and health, with help as necessary from the relevant public authorities. The underlying principle behind this shift is perhaps best expressed in the Robens Report on occupational health and safety in Great Britain which states that the "primary responsibility for doing something about the present levels of occupational accidents and diseases lies with those who create the risks and those who work with them", it being recognised that supervision external to the undertaking can never be as effective as measures taken voluntarily by employers and workers. Emphasis is, therefore, on self-regulation and on the sense of responsibility and the level of commitment of the social partners.

It should be noted, in the context of this guide, that although the legislation in many industrialised countries and even in some developing countries now prescribes in some detail the rights and obligations of employers, the role of managers – where they are not synonymous with employers – and of supervisory staff (e.g. heads of departments, services and workshops, supervisors and foremen) though sometimes mentioned is not usually the subject of specific provisions except in a few countries. It is, however, implicit in so far as management is responsible for carrying out the employers' policies and fulfilling their duties and obligations at the level of the workplace. This was recognised by a spokesman for the International Organisation of Employers in a report to an international seminar on occupational safety policies held in Turin in 1976, when he stated that "the employer ... [who] must have primary responsibility for the prevention of accidents" must in practice "delegate this [responsibility] through the chain of line management and make the necessary arrangements for a clear definition of responsibility for safety at each management level down to the supervision of the workplace". Thus it is clear that the term "employer" as used in the ILO's standards can apply equally – especially at the level of the enterprise – to managerial staff at various levels.

The general principle of management responsibility in this field was outlined as early as 1929 in the Recommendation concerning the prevention of industrial accidents (No. 31), which stated that –

> ... it is the duty of the employer to equip and manage his undertaking in such a way that the workers are adequately protected ... as well as to see that the workers in his employment are instructed as to the dangers, if any, of their occupation and in the measures to be covered by them in order to avoid accidents.

Since then a number of ILO standards have been formulated which reiterate this principle and which outline the employer's obligations at the level of the enterprise vis-à-vis physical conditions of work and the provision of a safe working environment. These provisions are summed up in Convention No. 155 which, in general terms, calls on employers to –

(1) ensure that ... the workplaces, machinery, equipment and processes under their control are safe and without risk to health;

(2) ensure that ... the chemical, physical and biological substances and agents under their control are without risk to health when appropriate measures are taken; and

(3) provide, where necessary, adequate protective clothing and protective equipment to prevent ... risk of accident or of adverse effects on health.

Recommendation No. 31 itself also calls for "the systematic" supervision of the works, machinery and plant for the purpose of ensuring safety and, in particular, of seeing that all safeguards and other safety appliances are maintained in proper order and position.

In practice what employers and managers are called upon to do involves a far wider range of actions than is apparent at first glance. For example, the obligation to ensure that workplaces, machinery, equipment and processes are safe and that the chemical, physical, biological substances and agents used are without risk to health should ideally involve such factors as: the design of plants and processes with a view to optimising conditions in the workplace and eliminating potential elements of risk; the careful choice of technologies and processes; the location and layout of premises; the planning of work stations; the choice of systems and work procedures; and the organisation of work (particularly in respect of hours of work and rest breaks and the elimination of excessive physical and mental fatigue). In short, these factors involve and influence the entire range of quality of working life issues which have preoccupied a number of countries since the late 1960s. More traditionally, the implementation of these provisions and those of Recommendation No. 97, concerning the protection of the health of workers in places of employment, would also cover the elimination, or at least the control, of physical hazards (such as noise, vibration, air pollution, ionising and non-ionising radiation) and chemical hazards (such as toxic substances).

Employers' organisations often actively encourage enterprises to transform the working environment and "enable the worker to give the best of himself without damage to his physical or mental integrity" based on the conviction already suggested earlier, that humanity and profitability go hand in hand. In fact, it is the policy of many employers' organisations to keep managers informed regarding safety and health and to encourage them to keep safety considerations in mind even when manufacturing processes are still only at the planning stage.

Similarly, supervision for the purpose of ensuring the maintenance of plant and equipment is certainly a vital function, since even normal wear and tear, if uncorrected, can have negative effects on safety and health and can lead to a deterioration of the working environment in that it entails additional effort and strain or added risks for the operators. Preventive maintenance is indeed an important factor in the elimination of occupational accidents. Moreover, the supervision envisaged by Recommendation No. 31 also entails the supervision of work and work practices (undoubtedly a management function) and of the application and use of occupational safety and health measures either by management or by specially appointed safety officers. The maintenance of personal protective equipment required by the Occupational Health Services Recommendation, 1959, might also be considered part of this function.

In general terms, even leaving aside the obvious benefits in terms of the safety and health of workers and the consequent reduction in costs which might otherwise accrue in terms of medical services, compensation and possible penalties, the maintenance of plant and equipment while possibly – though not necessarily – involving more work for supervisory staff and line management, makes sound economic sense in the long term.

Safety and health training

Instruction and training of workers at the level of the enterprise should form an integral part of any workplace safety and health programme and many of the ILO's instruments carry reference to this managerial responsibility – which should not, however, be confused with "information" for workers' safety representatives and other bodies, for which provision is also made. Recommendation No. 31, for example, calls for the explanation to new, and especially young, workers of the possible dangers of work and of the machinery or plant connected with their work. Recommendation No. 97 stipulates that workers should be informed of the necessity of the measures of protection; of their obligation to co-operate and of their obligation to make proper use of protective appliances and equipment. Similarly, Recommendation No. 164 suggests that employers should give the necessary instruction and training to workers, taking into account the functions and capacities of different categories of workers. The rationale behind this insistence on training regarding safey and health practices and protective measures and equipment (and of the eventual utility of this service to management which is required to provide it) is elaborated in Recommendation No. 31, which suggests that "in view of the fact that workers, by their conduct in the factory, can and should contribute to a large extent to the success of protective measures ... employers should do all in their power to improve the education of their workers in regard to the prevention of accidents". In short, a worker who is fully alive to the dangers inherent in his job is far more likely to take the necessary precautions to avoid accidents and is also more likely to co-operate in the use and maintenance of the protective equipment provided by the employer.

It might be of interest to note here that one recent study demonstrates that workplace safety rules can become an integral component of the system of management control and thus an alienating factor in the workplace – a result which could be avoided if workers were themselves involved in the discussion and analysis of problems and the formulation of the rules and procedures which make up the body of these regulations. Several countries have experimented with such involvement through project groups and research terms and it has been suggested that participative training (i.e. training which involves the participants in real life investigations by confronting them with specific problems whose characteristics, structure and applicable solutions they should be able to discover (for themselves)) could make a useful contribution to safety at the workplace.

Occupational health services in the enterprise

The provision of occupational health services in places of employment is an essential component of any programme concerned with the safety and health of workers and the improvement of the working environment. The ILO provides comprehensive guide-lines for the setting up of such services in its Recommendation concerning occupational health services in places of employment, 1959 (No. 112).

Basically, the Recommendation provides for the establishment of such a service "in or near a place of employment" for the purposes of –

(a) protecting the workers against any health hazards which may arise out of their work or the conditions in which it is carried on;

(b) contributing towards the workers' physical and mental adjustment, in particular by the adaptation of work to the workers and their assignment to jobs for which they are suited; and

(c) contributing to the establishment and maintenance of the highest possible degree of physical and mental well-being of the workers.

Managers are concerned in the setting up of such services in so far as the Recommendation provides that those services should be organised by enterprises for themselves individually or as a service common to a number of enterprises.

As outlined in Recommendation No. 112, the functions of occupational health services reflect the wider concept of occupational safety and health embodied in Convention No. 155 and reflected by other recent ILO activities in the area of working conditions and the working environment. In particular, it stipulates that the functions of these services should include inquiry into and analysis of the factors which lead to illnesses so that they are better able to evaluate the existing preventive programmes and discover occupational hazards. Their functions are also to include:

- surveillance of factors which may affect the health of workers, and advice to management in this respect;
- job analysis in the light of hygiene, physiological and *psychological* consider-ations and advice to management and workers on the best possible adaptation of jobs to workers (and not vice versa as has been customary, and still is in many countries);
- participation in the prevention of accidents and occupational diseases and supervision of personal protective equipment;
- carrying out the various medical examinations provided for in the Recommen-dation; and
- the provision of emergency treatment and first aid.

As an examination of these functions demonstrates, management can derive considerable benefit from the establishment of an occupational health service (over and above the obvious ones of emergency treatment and medical services) which could fully justify the economic costs it may entail.

In the first instance, through its inquiry into health-related absences, the occupational health service provides a very useful monitoring service which can alert managers to the existence of hazards and to gaps in the undertaking's preventive programme. Surveillance of factors affecting the health of workers serves the same function. In addition, the occupational health service is expected to serve as an expert advisory system for management and workers on a number of matters that are of crucial concern to occupational safety and health in the widest sense of the term, its job analysis functions being a case in point. The participation and advice of specialists in occupational medicine can add a valuable dimension to the manager's own work with regard to the prevention of accidents and, if efficient, the service's supervision of protective equipment and its use could reduce manage-ment's own obligations in this area while maintaining the safety and health of workers. Here again, the advice of experts in occupational medicine could be invaluable in the adaptation and improvement of protective equipment and methods. Finally, the records on work-related injuries and health problems which the service is expected to compile could be useful to the manager in regard to his obligations vis-à-vis the labour inspectorate.

In this regard it is interesting for managers to note that the Working Environment (Air Pollution, Noise and Vibration) Convention, 1977, provides that a competent person (or outside service) be appointed to deal with matters concern-ing the prevention and control of air pollution, noise and vibration in the working environment.

Rights and duties of workers

The rights and duties of workers under the provisions of the various international standards concerning occupational safety and health and the working environment have considerable implications for the work of managers.

While many of these provisions are sometimes seen by managers as an undue infringement on their prerogatives, the delineation of workers' actions at the level of the enterprise normally should not be considered as contrary to management's own interests. For example, Convention No. 155 calls on workers, in the course of performing their duties, to co-operate in the fulfilment by their employers of the obligations placed on them with regard to safety and health in the workplace. It further enjoins representatives of workers in the undertaking to co-operate with the employer in this field. In the same context it should be noted that the legislation of several countries now provides for the imposition of penalties on workers who fail to perform a legally required duty or who violate certain prohibitions in the field of safety and health.

It is, however, understandable that certain of the provisions of the Convention could appear to threaten management prerogatives and infringe on managers' traditional functions and decision-making powers. Article 19, for example, requires that there should be arrangements under which workers' representatives are given adequate information on existing safety and health measures and may consult with their organisations on these measures, are enabled to inquire into, and are consulted by the employer on all aspects of occupational health and safety associated with their work and may bring in technical advisers from the outside. The Article also requires that workers be given the right to refuse to work in situations which constitute a danger to their safety or health.

Article 20 of the Convention enlarges on this idea of the active involvement of workers and their representatives in the promotion of occupational safety and health at the workplace by stipulating that:

Co-operation between management and workers and/or their representatives within the undertaking shall be an essential element of organisational and other measures taken in pursuance of this Convention.

Although workers everywhere do not enjoy these rights and management's initial reaction to any efforts to provide them may have been one of opposition, there is, nevertheless, an increasing recognition of the fact that, in view of the growing complexity of work and of the working environment, the pooling of skills and efforts is indispensable and that workers, as well as employers, have a decisive role to play in the campaign against occupational risks. Workers' rights to information are now widely recognised; they are more frequently consulted and the scope of this consultation is widening. Provisions regarding their right to consult their representative organisations regarding management's safety and health measures and their right to bring in technical advisers from outside – both of which have been seen by some as threats to management – have built-in safeguards with regard, in the first case, to commercial secrets and, in the second, the choice (by mutual agreement) of technical advisers.

Perhaps what is considered by managers to be the most threatening of the provisions of Article 19 is, quite understandably, the workers' right to refuse to work, a right which some managers find to be open to abuse. However, where this right has been ceded to workers, experience has shown that managers' fears in this direction are largely unjustified and that workers are usually fully aware of the need to safeguard this right by its use only where extreme circumstances justify such an action. Indeed the Convention itself provides that a worker may have the right to refuse to return to a workplace only if there is continuing, imminent and serious danger to life or health.

In general terms, in so far as the workers' right to participate in the management of health protection at the workplace, implied in Articles 19 and 20 of Convention No. 155, is concerned, this is actually officially recognised in only a few countries and then in widely varying degrees ranging from consultation and co-determination (i.e. prior agreement or the right of veto) to direct autonomous management. However, there is much to be said for such a development and the recent experiences of some industrialised countries have demonstrated that if workers are given the right to information and consultation, the right to participate and the right to refuse dangerous work, they can influence the work environment quite significantly in a positive way. In these countries, notwithstanding initial fears and opposition of management in a number of cases, both social partners have come to recognise that their collaboration on this issue could constitute a valuable means of improving the working environment and assuring the safety and health of workers without jeopardising the well-being of the enterprise.

There are several arguments in favour of the active participation of workers in the promotion of occupational safety and health at the workplace which are of special interest to managers. In the first instance, giving workers an active role in safety and health implies a tremendous increase in the resources available to the undertaking for the implementation of its programme. Using the ideas, knowledge and experience of workers who are directly affected by the problems can make an invaluable contribution to identifying and overcoming them and provide for a basis of improvement which does not rely exclusively on the ability of a service external to the undertaking (e.g. the labour inspectorate) to understand all possible work situations and to provide blanket solutions to all problems. Today this is acknowledged as a major reason for enlarging participation in occupational safety and health. Participation could also constitute a valuable means of ensuring the active co-operation of workers in the promotion of safety and health, in that their involvement in these matters would make workers more conscious of the existence of hazards and would motivate them to comply with the safety regulations. This idea has been behind the ILO's own insistence on co-operation between the social partners in occupational safety and health, as is evidenced by the relevant provisions in Recommendations Nos. 31, 97 and 164 and Convention

No. 155. In addition, informed and alert workers are ideally situated to monitor potential hazards and give notice of imminent dangers.

Finally, it might be argued that the co-operation between employers and workers which is essential to the improvement of working conditions can only be achieved if it is based on partnership. In fact, this argument has led to a conclusion, which is current in a number of countries, that health protection is a matter not only for consultation but also, in appropriate cases, for negotiation and joint regulation. It should, however, be noted that this last point is sometimes challenged not only by managers but also by some unions which feel that negotiation would detract from what they consider management's moral obligation to provide a safe working environment.

Except in very small undertakings, it is clear that such participation in the promotion of occupational safety and health at the level of the workplace must, of necessity, take place through representatives, particularly when it entails influencing decision-makers on issues where the collective interests of all workers are involved. Institutional arrangements for such participation can be general, as in the case of existing institutions with a wider brief (such as works councils, staff representatives or union delegates); or they can constitute specialised mechanisms (such as work environment committees, safety committees and safety representatives). Specialised joint safety committees, many of which have existed since before the Second World War, often on a voluntary basis, must also be mentioned.

Experience in several countries has demonstrated that the latter type of mechanism (i.e. specialised bodies) are often more effective and a number of the countries which have recently revised their legislation on safety and health have encouraged the setting up of specialised institutions at various levels of the enterprise for the purpose of encouraging co-operation between the social partners. Examples include safety groups (Denmark) at the unit level, comprising supervisors and workers' safety representatives, safety committees (Denmark) and health and safety committees (France) at the plant level, and working conditions committees (Netherlands) and factory councils or environmental committees (Italy) comprising workers representing specific departments or elected by groups of workers subjected to similar working conditions.

The utility of such bodies lies in the fact that they relate specifically to safety and health issues and encourage participation to be as direct as possible, allowing the expertise of those exposed to certain working conditions to be brought to bear directly on existing or potential problems. Used effectively they could, in turn, serve as a useful mechanism whereby management can draw on the expertise of the workforce for the resolution of problems pertaining to the working environment and for the meeting of its own obligations vis-à-vis the State in this field. In addition, if mechanisms for participation are operative at the shop-floor level, the inspection and monitoring functions which should constitute an essential element of worker involvement could be far more effectively implemented. Specialised institutional arrangements have a further utility in that their specialised nature gives them a greater permanency and their work more continuity. In addition, the continual presence of members of such bodies on the shop floor allows for a far greater awareness and a tighter monitoring of potential problem areas than is possible in the case of more generalised bodies. The experience of certain of the more advanced countries suggests that such committees can be used very effectively to promote occupational safety and health in the workplace to the mutual benefit of both management and the workforce.

One final recent innovation in co-operation and participation in safety and health questions which could usefully be mentioned is the constitution by some countries of permanent research teams for the improvement of working conditions on the shop floor in order to "encourage the men on the shop floor to uncover problems that arise at their level with a view to seeking and propos-ing concrete solutions". Members are drawn from different levels of personnel ranging from engineers to rank-and-file workers. The teams are invaluable to management not only because they serve the useful function of methodically carrying out studies on occupational hazards and proposing concrete sugges-tions on which management can act, but also because they encourage the direct expression of workers' views in the undertaking – a factor which, incidentally, may be viewed with suspicion by some trade unions which, if they are not in-volved, may see it as a management ploy for reducing their own influence in the workplace.

Thus a happy but not entirely expected effect of the promotion of workers' participation at the workplace has been a growing trade union interest in safety and health issues, an interest which has expressed itself in increasing union activity in this field. Of undoubted interest to managers is the unions' involve-ment in safety education and training, sometimes in collaboration with employers. In some countries the unions also actively encourage their members to participate in management-sponsored safety education programmes. In others they themselves organise training courses for safety representatives. The success of the latter and their indirect benefit to management is amply demon-strated by the fact that, in one country, a number of line managers reported recently that they rely on union-trained safety representatives as their primary source of safety and health information.

* * *

Occupational hazards change continuously with the progress of indus-trialisation and with advances in technology. While some hazards are elimin-ated, or at least contained, by new machinery and work processes and by increasing awareness and knowledge of potentially dangerous substances and processes, the increasing complexity of work has given rise to new problems, created new tensions, frustrations and dissatisfaction and has led – as managers themselves have noted – to absenteeism and a decline in the quality of production.

Thus, the prevention of occupational hazards and the creation of a safe working environment and an adequate quality of working life requires, in its turn, constant attention, adaptation and innovation, a process in which both social partners have a role to play.

Legislation on the international and national levels will provide the guide-lines for their activities but it is impossible, in a constantly changing work environment, to formulate safeguards against every possible hazardous situation which can arise. For this reason, and since supervision and monitoring by services external to the undertaking can never be as effective as measures taken voluntarily by employers and workers, the social partners must collaborate in providing a safe and healthy working environment which caters to the physical, mental and social needs of their workers.

The participation of workers, directly and through representatives, is a key to this collaboration and is not just more equitable socially but can be justified economically on the grounds that a better quality of working life has been known to have a positive effect on absenteeism, quality, productivity and job satisfaction. It is, therefore, in the manager's long-term economic interest to encourage worker involvement in the promotion of occupational safety and health and the creation of a safe and healthy working environment.

Chapter 9

The manager and the personnel function

For centuries, organisations have been concerned with human problems, but only very recently has the importance of the personnel function become evident at the highest level. It cannot be too strongly emphasised at this point that personnel management is in no way the exclusive domain of the personnel department or the personnel manager. All members of management – from the highest to the lowest level – are responsible for the personnel function, and they all must understand that function, and the methods of dealing with personnel problems and situations. In particular, line management must work closely with the personnel staff in the interest of effective management of human resources. Both line management and personnel staff must share the responsibility for handling human problems. First line supervisors who deal directly with the workers in carrying out their own assignment have the greatest responsibility for personnel management and the greatest effect on the outcome of the implementation of personnel policies. But they are not alone and they need the firm support of higher management, including top management.

International labour standards, by their very nature, cannot give very detailed guide-lines for the carrying out of the personnel function. There are, however, certain important elements of this function upon which international instruments touch. In this chapter personnel areas related to international standards which will be discussed include aspects of the employment process (recruitment, selection and placement); grievance procedures; termination of employment; wage and benefit administration; and the development of human resources. Other aspects of the personnel function, such as relations with trade unions and consultation and communications, have been dealt with separately above.

The employment process (recruitment, selection and placement)

The employment process involves finding needed workers for the enterprise and seeing that they are placed in the right job. It also involves settling the new worker in his job and lateral and upward movement of the worker during his career. Finally, the employment process involves termination of the services of the worker, but this aspect will be considered in a separate section of this chapter.

"Recruitment" and "selection" refer to identifying sources of future employees (e.g. through employment exchanges, advertisements, notices at or outside the workplace, proposals of current employees, etc.) and choosing those applicants to be engaged (through formal or informal interviews, reference checks, tests, etc.). "Placement", sometimes merged into selection, can be a separate process of fitting selected job applicants to particular jobs (where they are not selected initially to fill particular job openings). "Induction" – which will not be dealt with here – refers to the orientation and initial instructions given to the new employee. "Promotion" and "transfer" need no explanation.

The recruitment and selection of a worker constitutes the beginning of the employment relationship. It is a moment in which management should act with care since the engagement of personnel can imply certain lasting obligations for the enterprise; it is also a moment of cardinal importance in the life of the worker.

A series of international instruments which deal with employment policies and employment services and agencies will not be discussed here since they are not of direct relevance to managers' immediate concerns in the enterprise. Of direct relevance, however, are the Convention and Recommendation concerning discrimination in respect of employment and occupation, 1958, since these have an immediate and direct impact on the employment process. While these instruments are primarily directed at promoting appropriate government policies, such policies have an obvious and direct influence on the employment policies adopted, and the employment practices utilised, by managers.

The general thrust of the Convention is the prevention of discrimination that "has the effect of nullifying or impairing equality of opportunity or treatment in employment or occupation". Discrimination refers to "any distinction, exclusion or preference on the basis of race, colour, sex, religion, political opinion, nationality, or social origin". The inherent requirements of a particular job, however, may make it necessary to make distinctions or give preference to persons who meet these requirements. In such a case there is no discrimination in the sense of the Convention. For instance, there would not necessarily be discrimination if persons of a particular religion were preferred for employment in a religious establishment. Nor would there necessarily be discrimination if women were excluded from jobs that, because of strength, or sexual particularities, were deemed to be suitable only for a male employee. However, particularly with regard to sex-based preferences in recruitment and selection, it must be said that the idea of "reserved jobs" is undergoing considerable change in national law and practice.

However, to promote equality of opportunity it may be necessary for a certain period to discriminate "positively" and give preference to representatives of minority groups or groups which are under-represented. For example, the ILO Committee of Experts found no problem of conformity with these standards where government policy called for giving temporary preferential treatment to women in the case of equivalent candidates for employment in the civil service in cases in which the existing distribution of functions between men and women in the unit concerned or within the organisation as a whole warrants such preference.

The discrimination instruments thus insist that employers and managers not practise or countenance discrimination in engaging or training of employees, in questions of promotion or in fixing terms and conditions of employment (remuneration questions are discussed elsewhere in this guide). Employers (as well as trade unions) are also called upon to ensure that the principle of equality of opportunity and non-discrimination be respected in collective bargaining and, more generally, in labour-management relations.

It may be noted that, in addition to the reservations mentioned earlier, the instruments stress that their provisions are not intended to prejudice special measures of protection or assistance generally recognised as necessary for specific groups (by virtue of, for example, sex, age, disablement, family responsibilities or social or cultural status). More specifically the Convention refers in this regard to special measures of protection or assistance contained in other ILO instruments.

In regard to the employment process, at least a passing reference should be made to the Vocational Rehabilitation and Employment (Disabled Persons) Convention (No. 159) and Recommendation (No. 168), both of 1983. In particular the Recommendation provides that disabled persons should enjoy equality of opportunity and treatment as regards access to jobs as well as retention and advancement in employment. But such equality of opportunity, under the Recommendation, is to take account of the suitability of particular disabled persons for the employment or jobs concerned. Moreover, "positive discrimination" is also referred to by the Recommendation when it states that special positive measures aimed at effective equality of opportunity and treatment between disabled and other workers should not be regarded as discrimination against other workers.

Other international standards with a bearing on the employment process in enterprises are Convention No. 156 and Recommendation No. 165 concerning equal opportunities and equal treatment for men and women workers: workers with family responsibilities, 1981. Although the provisions are primarily directed at governments, they are certainly of relevance to managers in carrying out the personnel function.

Briefly stated, the relevant portions of the instruments provide that family responsibilities (or marital status) should not be a valid reason for refusal (or termination) of employment.

The Recommendation, among other things, also recognises the importance for such workers of measures aimed at improving working conditions and the quality of working life, and that such measures enable workers to reconcile their job and family responsibilities. Measures can include the progressive reduction of working hours and the introduction of more flexible working schedules and working arrangements (including shift work). The Recommendation also sets forth the principle of "parental" leave and leave of absence in case of illness of a child. While the adoption of, or respect for, such policies by managers can involve, in some cases, a need for careful planning and organisational flexibility, these can be compensated for by a workforce that is both more productive and, perhaps, more amenable to needed adjustments in the enterprise called for by changing economic and technological conditions.

Grievance procedures

Another important element of the personnel function has to do with grievances. Grievance procedures, whether unilaterally established by managers or resulting from negotiations or consultations with workers' representatives, are always a key aspect of the management of people and, hence, of the personnel function.

But what are grievances? In certain labour-management relations systems, little if any distinction is made between grievances and other forms of disputes or worker protest. However, the strong weight of universal practice would consider grievances as referring to complaints by a worker – or group of workers – based on a measure by management or a situation in the enterprise which they consider inconsistent with their terms and conditions of employment, as contained in applicable collective agreements, individual employment contracts, legislation, works rules, or custom and usage.

Since grievances that are not resolved, or at least given attention, can lead to widespread unrest and poor morale, with consequent effects on productive efficiency, knowledgeable managers recognise the importance of effective grievance procedures. And these managers will ensure that such procedures are introduced, whether in the context of collective bargaining or independently of collective bargaining. But grievance procedures can serve other ends of benefit to astute managers. By tracing sources and patterns of grievances, the manager can locate questionable practices or areas of discontent in the enterprise and undertake measures to correct or alleviate them. Moreover, analysing grievances can help managers to prepare their collective bargaining agenda.

Certain "guide-lines" for grievance handling are included in a Recommendation (No. 130) concerning the examination of grievances within the undertaking with a view to their settlement, which was adopted in 1967.

The main general principle established in this Recommendation is that a worker, acting individually or jointly with other workers, should have the right to submit a grievance without suffering any prejudice and to have this grievance examined pursuant to an appropriate procedure.

When a grievance procedure is established by agreement with the union, the Recommendation envisages, as good practice, that this procedure should obviate the need to have recourse to other measures – such as direct action – by calling for the parties to agree to abstain "from any action which might impede [its] effective functioning". The concerned trade unions or workers' representatives should be associated in the setting up and implementation of grievance procedures. It is interesting that the Recommendation recognises the importance of a sound personnel policy in minimising the number of grievances.

As a general rule grievance procedures, according to the Recommendation, should provide for an initial attempt at settlement directly between the worker concerned and his immediate supervisor. If such an attempt fails, the case may be examined at one or more higher levels, depending on the nature and size of the enterprise. The procedure should be as informal and rapid as possible, and the worker should have the right to be assisted by his union, a workers' representative in the undertaking or another person. The worker concerned and his representative should be allowed sufficient time off to participate in the procedure without loss of remuneration. The instrument also urges that the rules and practices governing the grievance procedure be brought to the knowledge of the employees.

In point of fact it is rare, these days, to find an enterprise, other than the smallest ones, without some sort of grievance procedure. However, inspired by the provisions of the relevant ILO standards, managers should ensure that the grievance procedures that they develop, unilaterally or jointly with workers' representatives, are effective ones that can serve the purpose of promoting harmony and constructive labour relations in the enterprise.

Termination of employment

There are few managerial acts more dramatic and more serious than that of terminating the employment of workers in the enterprise. Here we are speaking of dismissal, whatever the reason – or lack of reason – may be. And we are speaking of dismissals which may be a disciplinary measure by management or which may result from presumed incompetence or inability of the employees concerned or, finally, dismissals – including suspensions or lay-offs – which may result from changes in the economic and operational situation of the enterprise.

In most cases termination of employment at the initiative of the employer was long considered a unilateral and often unquestioned (and unquestionable) management prerogative. Perhaps coupled with the idea of "termination at will" was a requirement of a notice period or payment in lieu of such notice period. But such requirement did not really challenge the basic liberty of management to terminate at will – it merely put a (frequently minimal) price tag on that liberty.

However, the last quarter of a century – and longer in the case of certain countries – has seen the development of a degree of protection of employees against unjustified dismissal. What the term "unjustified" means in given cases is often the subject of discussion and will be explored below. But it is important to note here that this modification of the idea of termination at will has come about at times through collective agreement and, perhaps more frequently, through legislation. Sometimes, although cases are rather rare, protection against unjustified dismissal has resulted from employer initiatives and is embodied in works rules or supervisory handbooks.

Whatever the origins, source or motivation, an international consensus was built up in the early 1960s calling for some limitations on the unfettered possibilities of management to dismiss employees. In fact there developed in some countries restrictions on dismissal that were so severe as to lead employers and managers to complain that employees were being given absolute job security to the detriment of the viability of the enterprise which, it was argued, in turn prejudiced the economic health of the national economy.

In 1963, in response to these developments and in order to balance the interests of workers and enterprises, the International Labour Conference adopted a Recommendation (No. 119) concerning termination of employment at the initiative of the employer, providing for the guidance of governments, employers and workers in the vital and delicate area of job security.

Since then considerable changes have taken place in the law and practice of many countries. In the light of more recent developments, the Conference adopted in 1982 a Convention (No. 158) and Recommendation (No. 166) concerning termination of employment at the initiative of the employer. As will be seen, both the superseded Recommendation as well as the newer instruments seek to give protection to workers without jeopardising the situation of enterprises, but also seek to suggest a number of practices which can help to reduce or resolve problems arising out of a situation in which management feels constrained to dismiss employees or reduce the size of the workforce.

The Convention and Recommendation, as an initial matter, both provide for the possibility of excluding from all or some of their provisions certain categories of employees, that is those engaged for a specific period of time or for a specified task, those serving a period of probation or a qualifying period of employment (provided the period had been determined in advance and is of reasonable duration) and casual or short-term employees. However, the Convention provides that provision may be made to ensure that fixed-term or fixed-task employment contracts are really such and are not merely entered into to avoid the protection otherwise afforded.

The substantive provisions of the Convention and Recommendation are divided into standards of general application and supplementary provisions concerning termination of employment for economic, technological, structural or similar reasons. According to the basic principle on justification, the employment of an employee is not to be terminated unless there is a valid reason connected with his capacity or conduct or based on the operational requirements of the enterprise. Here should be noted again the concern shown by the instruments for the viability of the enterprise. This concern is further underscored by the supplementary provisions on workforce reductions. Several reasons are listed that are not to constitute valid reasons for termination, including trade union membership or participation in union activities (see Chapters 3 and 4).

In an interesting paragraph which reflects widespread personnel practice regarding disciplinary matters, the Recommendation provides that dismissal for misconduct should take place only after appropriate written warnings have been given where national law or practice would justify dismissal for repeated acts of the type in question. In a similar vein, the Recommendation provides that in cases of alleged unsatisfactory performance, the employee concerned should have been given appropriate instructions and written warning with no improvement shown within a reasonable period, if the dismissal is to be justified. In both of the cases mentioned, the employee may be assisted by another person.

The instruments provide for the right of an employee who considers that he has been unjustifiably terminated to appeal against that termination within a reasonable time to an impartial body (unless the termination had been previously authorised by a competent authority). In the appeal procedure, the instruments recognise that it can be difficult for the employee to prove that he did nothing to justify the termination. Thus provision is made for one or both of the following possibilities: the burden of providing the existence of a valid reason may rest with the employer, or the competent appeal body may "reach a conclusion on the reason for the termination having regard to the evidence provided by the parties and according to the procedures provided for by national law and practice".

If found to be unjustified, the termination may be invalid or reinstatement ordered. However, payment of adequate compensation may be the remedy if reinstatement or retention of the employee is not provided for nationally or if such measures are deemed impracticable by the appeals body.

Additional provisions of the instruments deal with period of notice, certificates of employment, severance allowance and other income protection.

The supplementary provisions concerning termination of employment for economic, technological or structural reasons call upon the employer foreseeing such terminations to inform and consult with workers' representatives on possible measures to avert or minimise the terminations and measures to mitigate their adverse effects. It is significant to note that the Recommendation emphasises that measures to avert or minimise terminations should not be such as to prejudice the efficient operation of the enterprise. Again, the instruments seek to achieve a balance between the diverse interests at stake.

In fact the Recommendation cites a number of measures which could be considered to avert termination. These include restrictions on hiring, gradual reduction over a certain period to allow natural attrition to operate, transfers, retraining, voluntary early retirements, overtime restrictions and reduction of normal working hours.

The Recommendation further calls for pre-established criteria to be used in deciding on those to be terminated in a workforce reduction, but provides that these criteria should take into account the interest of both the enterprise and the employees. In practice these criteria often include, on the one hand, relative skill, ability, experience and qualifications of individual employees coupled with the needs of the enterprise for its continued efficiency and, on the other hand, highly objective factors such as length of service, age and family situation. It is not without interest that while the original Termination of Employment Recommendation of 1963 explicitly cited the above criteria, the newer Recommendation (which supersedes the 1963 instrument) refrains from any enumeration, contenting itself to mention the general principle of pre-established criteria which, as mentioned above, give due regard to the interests of the enterprise.

Additional provisions of the Recommendation call for a priority of re-engagement – which may be limited to a specified time period – for workers who had been terminated in a contraction of the workforce for economic, technological or structural reasons, if the enterprise again hires workers. Once again, the instrument seeks to give consideration to the needs of the enterprise by specifying that re-engagement may be limited to former employees having the necessary qualifications.

One not infrequently hears the complaint from managers that in matters of termination of employees, they lack the flexibility necessary to run the enterprise efficiently. This may or may not be so in cases where national laws or regulations (or even collective agreements "voluntarily" entered into) have rigid and ill-conceived provisions in this regard. But the relevant ILO standards discussed above could and should inspire national practice – and even that at the enterprise level – that has sufficient in-built flexibility to afford the enterprise the leeway and freedom that efficiency dictates and to afford employees protection against unfair or arbitrary treatment. And managers should remember that fairness and consideration does not hurt morale in the workforce and that good morale does not hurt productivity.

Development of human resources

An important aspect of the personnel function concerns the training and development of human resources, including the training of managers. Convention No. 142 and Recommendation No. 150, both adopted in 1975, deal with vocational guidance and vocational training in the development of human resources.

Training, as a function of personnel management, obviously has great advantages for the enterprise, and managers are increasingly instituting enterprise-level training wherever possible and even on a fairly modest scale. It is more and more recognised that enterprise training plans, programmes and policies can "provide a firm basis for greater job mobility, for a greater degree of adaptability to changing patterns of work, product mix and technology" and for career planning. As with measures for humanisation of work discussed earlier, an effective training programme can result in a "double pay-off" of increased employee satisfaction and increased productivity through effective manpower utilisation.

Thus the Recommendation calls on enterprises to assume responsibility for training their employees and urges managers to co-operate with workers' representatives when planning training programmes (which should be co-ordinated, as necessary, with the public training system).

Reference is made in the instrument to induction for new jobholders to familiarise them with the nature and objectives of the enterprise and the conditions under which they are expected to perform their work.

The Recommendation also calls for systematic complementary training on the job by enterprises and, in particular, further training plans. Above all, these plans should provide employees with the opportunity to qualify for advancement to higher level skills and responsibilities. Employees undergoing training in the enterprise should receive adequate remuneration or allowances.

Another point to be noted under the heading of development of human resources refers to disabled persons. The Vocational Rehabilitation and Employment (Disabled Persons) Recommendation, 1983 (No. 168), calls on employers' and workers' representatives in enterprises to co-operate (along with specialists), wherever possible, in examining the possibilities for vocational rehabilitation and job reallocation of disabled workers in the enterprise. In fact, under the Recommendation, enterprises are encouraged, where possible, to have their own vocational rehabilitation services, including sheltered employment.

The Human Resources Development Recommendation, 1975 (No. 150), contains an important section on training for managers and supervisors, that is for those " in charge of the work of others, for professional and specialist personnel participating in management and for persons being prepared to assume management and supervisory functions". The Recommendation suggests that management training programmes aim at: (i) developing an understanding of the economic and social aspects of decision-making; (ii) fostering abilities for leading and motivating other persons and for developing sound industrial relations; (iii) developing a positive attitude towards change and an appreciation of the effect of change on people; (iv) developing a capacity to assume new responsibilities on the job; (v) developing an awareness of the importance of education and vocational training for the personnel of the undertaking; (vi) developing a concern for the welfare of workers and a knowledge of labour law and social security schemes; and finally, (vii) developing an understanding of the value of efforts towards self-improvement.

In this respect, it may be worthwhile to recall that management education and training could be facilitated through paid educational leave arrangements as provided for by Convention No. 140, discussed above.

Appendix: international labour Conventions and Recommendations currently in force

I. Basic human rights

(a) Freedom of association

Convention No. 11: Right of Association (Agriculture), 1921

Convention No. 87: Freedom of Association and Protection of the Right to Organise, 1948

Convention No. 98: Right to Organise and Collective Bargaining, 1949

Convention No. 135: Workers' Representatives, 1971

Recommendation No. 143: Workers' Representatives, 1971

Convention No. 141: Rural Workers' Organisations, 1975

Recommendation No. 149: Rural Workers' Organisations, 1975

Convention No. 151: Labour Relations (Public Service), 1978

Recommendation No. 159: Labour Relations (Public Service), 1978

See also: Convention No. 84, Convention No. 110, Parts IX and X, and under II: Labour Relations.

(b) Forced labour

Convention No. 29: Forced Labour, 1930

Recommendation No. 35: Forced Labour (Indirect Compulsion), 1930

Convention No. 104: Abolition of Forced Labour, 1957

See also: Recommendation No. 136.

(c) Equality of opportunity and treatment

Convention No. 100: Equal Remuneration, 1951

Recommendation No. 90: Equal Remuneration, 1951

Convention No. 111: Discrimination (Employment and Occupation), 1958

Recommendation No. 111: Discrimination (Employment and Occupation), 1958

Convention No. 156: Workers with Family Responsibilities, 1981

Recommendation No. 165: Workers with Family Responsibilities, 1981

See also: Convention No. 82, Part VI, Convention No. 117, Part V.

II. Employment

(a) Employment policy

Convention No. 2: Unemployment, 1919

Convention No. 122: Employment Policy, 1964

Recommendation No. 122: Employment Policy, 1964

Recommendation No. 136: Special Youth Schemes, 1970

(b) Employment services and agencies

Convention No. 34: Fee-Charging Employment Agencies, 1933

Convention No. 88: Employment Service, 1948
Recommendation No. 83: Employment Service, 1948
Convention No. 96: Fee-Charging Employment Agencies (Revised), 1949

(c)   Employment security
Recommendation No. 119: Termination of Employment, 1963
See also: Convention No. 137, Recommendation No. 145, Convention No. 145, Recommendation No. 154.

III. Social policy

Convention No. 117: Social Policy (Basic Aims and Standards), 1962
Recommendation No. 127: Co-operatives (Developing Countries), 1966
See also: Convention No. 82.

IV. Labour administration

See also under II *(b):* Employment services and agencies
(a)   General
Convention No. 150: Labour Administration, 1978
Recommendation No. 158: Labour Administration, 1978
See also: Recommendation No. 113.

(b)   Labour inspection
Convention No. 81: Labour Inspection, 1947
Recommendation No. 81: Labour Inspection, 1947
Recommendation No. 82: Labour Inspection (Mining and Transport), 1947
Convention No. 129: Labour Inspection (Agriculture), 1969
Recommendation No. 133: Labour Inspection (Agriculture), 1969
See also: Recommendation No. 28, Convention No. 110, Part XI.

(c)   Labour statistics
Convention No. 63: Concerning Statistics of Wages and Hours of Work, 1938

(d)   Tripartite consultation
Convention No. 144: Tripartite Consultation (International Labour Standards), 1976
Recommendation No. 152: Tripartite Consultation (Activities of the International Labour Organisation), 1976

V. Labour relations

Recommendation No. 91: Collective Agreements, 1951
Recommendation No. 92: Voluntary Conciliation and Arbitration, 1951
Recommendation No. 94: Co-operation at the Level of the Undertaking, 1952
Recommendation No. 113: Consultation (Industrial and National Levels), 1960
Recommendation No. 129: Communications within the Undertaking, 1967 ,
Recommendation No. 130: Examination of Grievances, 1967
Convention No. 154: Collective Bargaining, 1981
Recommendation No. 163: Collective Bargaining, 1981
See also under I *(a): Freedom of association*

VI. Conditions of work

(a)   Wages

See also: Convention No. 82, Part V, Convention No. 110, Part IV, Convention No. 117, Part IV.

1.   Minimum wage-fixing machinery

Convention No. 26: Minimum Wage-Fixing Machinery, 1928

Convention No. 99: Minimum Wage-Fixing Machinery (Agriculture), 1951

Convention No. 131: Minimum Wage Fixing, 1970

Recommendation No. 135: Minimum Wage Fixing, 1970

2.   Protection of wages

Convention No. 95: Protection of Wages, 1949

Recommendation No. 85: Protection of Wages, 1949

3.   Labour clauses in public contracts

Convention No. 94: Labour Clauses (Public Contracts), 1949

Recommendation No. 84: Labour Clauses (Public Contracts), 1949

(b)   General conditions of employment

1.   Hours of work

Convention No. 1: Hours of Work (Industry), 1919

Convention No. 30: Hours of Work (Commerce and Offices), 1930

Convention No. 43: Sheet-Glass Works, 1934

Convention No. 46: Hours of Work (Coal Mines) (Revised), 1935

Convention No. 47: Forty-Hour Week, 1935

Convention No. 49: Reduction of Hours of Work (Glass-Bottle Works), 1935

Convention No. 51: Reduction of Hours of Work (Public Works), 1936

Convention No. 61: Reduction of Hours of Work (Textiles), 1937

Convention No. 67: Hours of Work and Rest Periods (Road Transport), 1939

Recommendation No. 116: Reduction of Hours of Work, 1962

Convention No. 153: Hours of Work and Rest Periods (Road Transport), 1979

Recommendation No. 161: Hours of Work and Rest Periods (Road Transport), 1979

See also: Recommendation No. 7, Convention No. 109, Part III, Recommendation No. 109.

2.   Night work

Convention No. 20: Night Work (Bakeries), 1925

See also under VIII *(b): Employment of women, night work;* IX *(b) Employment of children, night work*

3.   Weekly rest

Convention No. 14: Weekly Rest (Industry), 1921

Convention No. 106: Weekly Rest (Commerce and Offices), 1957

Recommendation No. 103: Weekly Rest (Commerce and Offices), 1957

See also: Convention No. 110, Part VI.

4.   Paid leave

Convention No. 52: Holidays with Pay, 1936

Recommendation No. 47: Holidays with Pay, 1936

Convention No. 101: Holidays with Pay (Agriculture), 1952

Recommendation No. 93: Holidays with Pay (Agriculture), 1952

Recommendation No. 98: Holidays with Pay, 1954
Convention No. 132: Holidays with Pay (Revised), 1970
Convention No. 140: Paid Educational Leave, 1974
Recommendation No. 148: Paid Educational Leave, 1974
See also: Convention No. 91, Convention No. 110, Part V, Convention No. 146.

(c) Occupational safety and health
1. General provisions
Recommendation No. 31: Prevention of Industrial Accidents, 1929
Recommendation No. 97: Protection of Workers' Health, 1953
Recommendation No. 112: Occupational Health Services, 1959
Convention No. 155: Occupational Safety and Health, 1981
Recommendation No. 164: Occupational Safety and Health, 1981
See also: Convention No. 110, Part XIII.

2. Protection against specific risks
– Toxic substances and agents
Recommendation No. 3: Anthrax Prevention, 1919
Recommendation No. 4: Lead Poisoning (Women and Children), 1919
Convention No. 13: White Lead (Painting), 1921
Convention No. 115: Radiation Protection, 1960
Recommendation No. 114: Radiation Protection, 1960
Convention No. 136: Benzene, 1971
Recommendation No. 144: Benzene, 1971
Convention No. 139: Occupational Cancer, 1974
Recommendation No. 147: Occupational Cancer, 1974
– Machinery
Convention No. 119: Guarding of Machinery, 1963
Recommendation No. 118: Guarding of Machinery, 1963
– Maximum weight
Convention No. 127: Maximum Weight, 1967
Recommendation No. 128: Maximum Weight, 1967
– Air pollution, noise and vibration
Convention No. 148: Working Environment (Air Pollution, Noise and Vibration), 1977
Recommendation No. 156: Working Environment (Air Pollution, Noise and Vibration), 1977

3. Protection in given branches of activity
– Building industry
Convention No. 62: Safety Provisions (Building), 1937
Recommendation No. 53: Safety Provisions (Building), 1937
Recommendation No. 55: Co-operation in Accident Prevention (Building), 1937
Recommendation No. 56: Vocational Education (Building), 1937
– Commerce and offices
Convention No. 120: Hygiene (Commerce and Offices), 1964
Recommendation No. 120: Hygiene (Commerce and Offices), 1964
– Dock work
Convention No. 27: Marking of Weight (Packages Transported by Vessels), 1929
Convention No. 28: Protection against Accidents (Dockers), 1929

Convention No. 32: Protection against Accidents (Dockers) (Revised), 1932
Convention No. 152: Occupational Safety and Health (Dock Work), 1979
Recommendation No. 160: Occupational Safety and Health (Dock Work), 1979
See also: Convention No. 134, Recommendation No. 142.

(d) Welfare
Recommendation No. 21: Utilisation of Spare Time, 1924
Recommendation No. 102: Welfare Facilities, 1956
Recommendation No. 115: Workers' Housing, 1961
See also: Convention No. 110, Part XII; and under XIV A and B: Seafarers – Safety, Health and Welfare.

VII. Social security

(a) Comprehensive standards
Recommendation No. 67: Income Security, 1944
Convention No. 102: Social Security (Minimum Standards), 1952
Convention No. 118: Equality of Treatment (Social Security), 1962
See also: Convention No. 70, Recommendation No. 75.

(b) Protection in the various social security branches
1. Medical care and sickness benefit
Convention No. 24: Sickness Insurance (Industry), 1927
Convention No. 25: Sickness Insurance (Agriculture), 1927
Recommendation No. 69: Medical Care, 1944
Convention No. 130: Medical Care and Sickness Benefits, 1969
Recommendation No. 134: Medical Care and Sickness Benefits, 1969
See also: Convention No. 55, Convention No. 56, Recommendation No. 76.

2. Old age, invalidity and survivors' benefits
Convention No. 35: Old-Age Insurance (Industry, etc.), 1933
Convention No. 36: Old-Age Insurance (Agriculture), 1933
Convention No. 37: Invalidity Insurance (Industry, etc.), 1933
Convention No. 38: Invalidity Insurance (Agriculture), 1933
Convention No. 39: Survivors' Insurance (Industry, etc.), 1933
Convention No. 40: Survivors' Insurance (Agriculture), 1933
Convention No. 48: Maintenance of Migrants' Pensions Rights, 1935
Convention No. 128: Invalidity, Old-Age and Survivors' Benefits, 1967
Recommendation No. 131: Invalidity, Old-Age and Survivors' Benefits, 1967
See also: Convention No. 71.

3. Employment injury benefit
Convention No. 12: Workmen's Compensation (Agriculture), 1921
Convention No. 17: Workmen's Compensation (Accidents), 1925
Recommendation No. 23: Workmen's Compensation (Jurisdiction), 1925
Convention No. 18: Workmen's Compensation (Occupational Diseases), 1925
Convention No. 19: Equality of Treatment (Accident Compensation), 1925
Recommendation No. 25: Equality of Treatment (Accident Compensation), 1925
Convention No. 42: Workmen's Compensation (Occupational Diseases) (Revised), 1934
Convention No. 121: Employment Injury Benefits, 1964

Recommendation No. 121: Employment Injury Benefits, 1964
See also: Convention No. 110, Part VIII.

4.   *Unemployment benefit*
Convention No. 44: Unemployment Provision, 1934
Recommendation No. 44: Unemployment Provision, 1934
See also: Convention No. 8, Recommendation No. 10.

5.   *Maternity benefit:* See under VIII *(a)*: *Maternity protection.*

VIII. Employment of women

See also under I (c)*:* Equality of opportunity and treatment

(a)   Maternity protection
Convention No. 3: Maternity Protection, 1919
Convention No. 103: Maternity Protection (Revised), 1952
Recommendation No. 95: Maternity Protection, 1952
See also: Convention No. 110, Part VII.

(b)   Night work
Convention No. 4: Night Work (Women), 1919
Recommendation No. 13: Night Work of Women (Agriculture), 1921
Convention No. 41: Night Work (Women) (Revised), 1934
Convention No. 89: Night Work (Women) (Revised), 1948

(c)   Underground work
Convention No. 45: Underground Work (Women), 1935

IX. Employment of children and young persons

(a)   Minimum age
Convention No. 5: Minimum Age (Industry), 1919
Convention No. 10: Minimum Age (Agriculture), 1921
Convention No. 33: Minimum Age (Non-Industrial Employment), 1932
Convention No. 59: Minimum Age (Industry) (Revised), 1937
Convention No. 60: Minimum Age (Non-Industrial Employment) (Revised), 1937
Convention No. 123: Minimum Age (Underground Work), 1965
Recommendation No. 124: Minimum Age (Underground Work), 1965
Convention No. 138: Minimum Age, 1973
Recommendation No. 146: Minimum Age, 1973
See also: Convention No. 7, Convention No. 15, Convention No. 58, Convention No. 112.

(b)   Night work
Convention No. 6: Night Work of Young Persons (Industry), 1919
Recommendation No. 14: Night Work of Children and Young Persons (Agriculture), 1921
Convention No. 79: Night Work of Young Persons (Non-Industrial Occupations), 1946
Recommendation No. 80: Night Work of Young Persons (Non-Industrial Occupations), 1946
Convention No. 90: Night Work of Young Persons (Industry) (Revised), 1948

(c)   Medical examination
Convention No. 77: Medical Examination of Young Persons (Industry), 1946
Convention No. 78: Medical Examination of Young Persons (Non-Industrial Occupations), 1946

Recommendation No. 79: Medical Examination of Young Persons, 1946
Convention No. 124: Medical Examination of Young Persons (Underground Work), 1965
See also: Convention No. 16.

(d)   Conditions of employment in underground work
Recommendation No. 125: Conditions of Employment of Young Persons (Underground Work), 1965

X. Older workers

Recommendation No. 162: Older Workers, 1980

XI. Migrant workers

Convention No. 21: Inspection of Emigrants, 1926
Convention No. 97: Migration for Employment (Revised), 1949
Recommendation No. 86: Migration for Employment (Revised), 1949
Recommendation No. 100: Protection of Migrant Workers (Underdeveloped Countries), 1955
Convention No. 143: Migrant Workers (Supplementary Provisions), 1975
Recommendation No. 151: Migrant Workers, 1975
See also: Convention No. 19, Convention No. 48, Convention No. 82, Part IV, Convention No. 110, Part II, Convention No. 117, Part III, Convention No. 118.

XII. Indigenous workers and tribal populations

Convention No. 50: Recruiting of Indigenous Workers, 1936
Recommendation No. 46: Elimination of Recruiting, 1936
Convention No. 64: Contracts of Employment (Indigenous Workers), 1939
Convention No. 65: Penal Sanctions (Indigenous Workers), 1939
Convention No. 86: Contracts of Employment (Indigenous Workers), 1947
Convention No. 104: Abolition of Penal Sanctions (Indigenous Workers), 1955
Convention No. 107: Indigenous and Tribal Populations, 1957
Recommendation No. 104: Indigenous and Tribal Populations, 1957

XIII. Workers in non-metropolitan territories

Recommendation No. 70: Social Policy in Dependent Territories, 1944
Recommendation No. 74: Social Policy in Dependent Territories (Supplementary Provisions), 1945
Convention No. 82: Social Policy (Non-Metropolitan Territories), 1947
Convention No. 83: Labour Standards (Non-Metropolitan Territories), 1947
Convention No. 84: Right of Association (Non-Metropolitan Territories), 1947
Convention No. 85: Labour Inspectorates (Non-Metropolitan Territories), 1947
See also under XII : *Indigenous workers and tribal populations*

XIV. Particular occupational sectors

(a)   Seafarers
1.   General
Recommendation No. 9: National Seamen's Codes, 1920

Recommendation No. 139: Employment of Seafarers (Technical Developments), 1970
Convention No. 145: Continuity of Employment (Seafarers), 1976
Recommendation No. 154: Continuity of Employment (Seafarers), 1976
Convention No. 147: Merchant Shipping (Minimum Standards), 1976
Recommendation No. 155: Merchant Shipping (Improvement of Standards), 1976

2.   *Training and entry into employment*
Convention No. 9: Placing of Seamen, 1920
Convention No. 22: Seamen's Articles of Agreement, 1926
Convention No. 108: Seafarers' Identity Documents, 1958
Recommendation No. 137: Vocational Training (Seafarers), 1970

3.   *Conditions for admission to employment*
Convention No. 7: Minimum Age (Sea), 1920
Convention No. 15: Minimum Age (Trimmers and Stokers), 1921
Convention No. 16: Medical Examination of Young Persons (Sea), 1921
Convention No. 58: Minimum Age (Sea) (Revised), 1936
Convention No. 73: Medical Examination (Seafarers), 1946
See also: Convention No. 138.

4.   *Certificates of competency*
Convention No. 53: Officers' Competency Certificates, 1936
Convention No. 69: Certification of Ships' Cooks, 1946
Convention No. 74: Certification of Able Seamen, 1946

5.   *General conditions of employment*
Convention No. 23: Repatriation of Seamen, 1926
Recommendation No. 27: Repatriation (Ship Masters and Apprentices), 1926
Convention No. 91: Paid Vacations (Seafarers) (Revised), 1949
Convention No. 109: Wages, Hours of Work and Manning (Sea) (Revised), 1958
Recommendation No. 109: Wages, Hours of Work and Manning (Sea), 1958
Convention No. 146: Seafarers' Annual Leave with Pay, 1976
Recommendation No. 153: Protection of Young Seafarers, 1976

6.   *Safety, health and welfare*
Recommendation No. 48: Seamen's Welfare in Ports, 1936
Convention No. 68: Food and Catering (Ships' Crews), 1946
Recommendation No. 78: Bedding, Mess Utensils and Miscellaneous Provisions (Ships' Crews), 1946
Convention No. 92: Accommodation of Crews (Revised), 1949
Recommendation No. 105: Ships' Medicine Chests, 1958
Recommendation No. 106: Medical Advice at Sea, 1958
Convention No. 133: Accommodation of Crews (Supplementary Provisions), 1970
Recommendation No. 138: Seafarers' Welfare, 1970
Recommendation No. 140: Crew Accommodation (Air Conditioning), 1970
Recommendation No. 141: Crew Accommodation (Noise Control), 1970
Convention No. 134: Prevention of Accidents (Seafarers), 1970
Recommendation No. 142: Prevention of Accidents (Seafarers), 1970

7.   *Labour inspection*
Recommendation No. 28: Labour Inspection (Seamen), 1926

8. Social security

Convention No. 8: Unemployment Indemnity (Shipwreck), 1920

Recommendation No. 10: Unemployment Insurance (Seamen), 1920

Convention No. 55: Shipowners' Liability (Sick and Injured Seamen), 1936

Convention No. 56: Sickness Insurance (Sea), 1936

Convention No. 70: Social Security (Seafarers), 1946

Recommendation No. 75: Seafarers' Social Security (Agreements), 1946

Recommendation No. 76: Seafarers (Medical Care for Dependents), 1946

Convention No. 71: Seafarers' Pensions, 1946

(b) Fishermen

Recommendation No. 7: Hours of Work (Fishing), 1920

Convention No. 112: Minimum Age (Fishermen), 1959

Convention No. 113: Medical Examination (Fishermen), 1959

Convention No. 114: Fishermen's Articles of Agreement, 1959

Convention No. 125: Fishermen's Competency Certificates, 1966

Convention No. 126: Accommodation of Crews (Fishermen), 1966

Recommendation No. 126: Vocational Training (Fishermen), 1966

(c) Inland boatmen

Recommendation No. 8: Hours of Work (Inland Navigation), 1920

(d) Dock workers

Convention No. 137: Dock Work, 1973

Recommendation No. 145: Dock Work, 1973

See also: Convention No. 27, Convention No. 28, Convention No. 32, Convention No. 152, Recommendation No. 160.

(e) Plantation workers

Convention No. 110: Plantations, 1958

Recommendation No. 110: Plantations, 1958

(f) Tenants and sharecroppers

Recommendation No. 132: Tenants and Sharecroppers, 1968

(g) Nursing personnel

Convention No. 149: Nursing Personnel, 1977

Recommendation No. 157: Nursing Personnel, 1977

XV. Training

Recommendation No. 99: Vocational Rehabilitation (Disabled), 1955

Convention No. 140: Paid Educational Leave, 1974

Recommendation No. 148: Paid Educational Leave, 1974

Convention No. 142: Human Resources Development, 1975

Recommendation No. 150: Human Resources Development, 1975

Convention No. 159: Vocational Rehabilitation and Employment (Disabled Persons), 1983

Recommendation No. 168: Vocational Rehabilitation and Employment (Disabled Persons), 1983

www.ingramcontent.com/pod-product-compliance
Lightning Source LLC
Chambersburg PA
CBHW071113210326
41519CB00020B/6281